The GARDENER'S YEAR

LONDON, NEW YORK, MUNICH, MELBOURNE, DELHI

Horticultural Consultant ❧ Veronica Peerless
Senior Editor ❧ Chauney Dunford
Project Art Editor ❧ Clare Marshall
Managing Editor ❧ Penny Warren
DK Picture Library ❧ Claire Cordier
Senior Jacket Creative ❧ Nicola Powling
Pre-production Producer ❧ Ray Williams
Senior Producer ❧ Ché Creasey
Art Director ❧ Jane Bull
Publisher ❧ Mary Ling

First published in Great Britain in 2014 by
Dorling Kindersley Limited
80 Strand, London, WC2R 0RL
Penguin Random House Group

Copyright © 2014 Dorling Kindersley Limited
2 4 6 8 10 9 7 5 3 1
001–184576–Sept/2014

A CIP catalogue record of this book is available from the British Library.

ISBN 978-1-4093-3985-4

Printed and bound in China by
Leo Paper Products Ltd

Discover more at
www.dk.com

The GARDENER'S YEAR

CONTENTS

FOUR SEASONS

Spring

The first flowers

It's thrilling to watch the garden finally wake up after a long, cold, and normally sodden, winter. It starts slowly, with a few green shoots and welcome early flowers peeping through the soil, and gradually builds into a joyful crescendo of colour. This is many gardeners' favourite season, ripe with fresh new growth and possibilities. It's also one of the busiest times. As the soil warms up and the days lengthen, there's the sowing, planting, pruning, and weeding to be done.

Bulbs are a vital part of the spring show, as the tiny, delicate blooms of irises and crocuses are followed by grape hyacinths, swathes of daffodils, and, finally, masses of colourful tulips.

If you have a tree that bears blossom in your garden, such as a magnolia, ornamental cherry, or crab apple, it will be the star of the show now. And some of our most spectacular shrubs, such as rhododendrons, camellias, and lilacs, put on a fantastic display in spring, too.

The earliest crops

Spring is a very busy time in the edible garden, as it's when seed sowing begins in earnest for harvests later in the year. But it's not all hard work. It's also a time to enjoy the first of your crops: tasty broad beans, the sweet spears of asparagus, and the earliest fruit crop of all, gooseberries.

You can also sow and eat speedy crops that are ready to harvest just a few weeks after sowing, such as salad leaves, baby beetroots, and radishes. Then, of course, there are the over-wintered crops, such as crisp kale and the hearty root vegetables.

IN THE GARDEN

Summer

Flourishing blooms

Summer is all about flowers, whether in containers, hanging baskets, or borders, and it's when most gardens are at their peak. Herbaceous perennials are now in the spotlight. Elegant spires of delphiniums, fleeting oriental poppies, glamorous peonies, and trusty hardy geraniums begin the show, followed by a riot of colour from phlox, penstemons, and African lilies. These are supported by attractive annuals that were sown in spring, such as cosmos, tagetes, and zinnias. Roses of all kinds are freely blooming, as are clematis and other climbers.

Tender bedding plants, such as pelargoniums, fuchsias, and petunias come to the fore, creating eye-catching spectacles in containers, hanging baskets, and windowboxes. You can also enjoy a bounty of cut flowers for the house, with sweet peas, cornflowers, and stocks, to name but a few.

There are still jobs to do in summer, such as watering, weeding, and deadheading, but don't forget to relax and enjoy your garden.

Edible abundance

The fruits of your labours in spring are rewarded now, as you begin harvesting delicious early new potatoes and garden peas, then French and runner beans, mange tout peas, courgettes, garlic and onions, and vibrant Swiss chard. It's also a productive time in the fruit garden, with tart

gooseberries, currants, and mountains of plump strawberries to enjoy, followed by cherries, blueberries, summer raspberries, and plums.

Autumn

The fiery finale

If summer is about flowers, autumn is about foliage, fruits, and berries. The leaves of many deciduous trees, climbers, and shrubs, such as maples, Boston ivy, and spindle tree, put on a fiery show before falling.

Meanwhile shrubs, such as cotoneaster and pyracantha, are smothered in berries, while shrub roses bear an abundance of bright red hips.

Of course, there are plenty of flowers to enjoy, too. Many annuals and perennials, such as cosmos and penstemon, will power on until the first frosts. In early autumn, colourful dahlias are at their peak, as are other exotic-looking plants, such as bananas, ginger lilies, and cannas. These are followed by perennial asters, in shades of white, purple, or blue, along with late-blooming nerines and chrysanthemums. This is also when ornamental grasses really come into their own, as their stems and plumes turn golden, bringing texture to the border, and complementing the seedheads of perennials that are now dying back.

It's the end of the growing season, but it's also a time to look ahead, too. Autumn is the time to plant new perennials, trees, and shrubs, as well as early bulbs for the spring to come.

A grand feast

Now is the time to enjoy the autumn bounty of sweetcorn, tomatoes, chillies, and aubergines; the last of the courgettes and beans; plus squashes and pumpkins. And there's fruit, too, such as apples and pears, to eat now or to store for later, along with autumn-fruiting raspberries that can continue cropping until the first proper frosts.

Winter

Cold comforts

Traditionally, borders were cut back or cleared in autumn, leaving them bare. Now many perennials and grasses are left standing over winter, as their shapes and forms bring interest to the garden, while providing food and habitat for wildlife. Winter is the season for evergreen foliage, colourful

stems, and interesting bark, as well as winter-flowering shrubs, many of which have a powerful scent. There are also winter bedding plants to enjoy, especially when planted near the house where they can be seen. And just as the year starts with bulbs, so it ends that way, with aconites and snowdrops that thrive grown *en masse* beneath deciduous trees and shrubs.

Cool crops

There's a surprising amount to harvest during winter, such as parsnips, cabbages, leeks, and kale, plus Brussels sprouts for Christmas dinner. Many can be left in the garden until you need them, and often taste better having been frosted.

ABOUT THIS BOOK

Organized by season, the plants and crops included are featured in the order in which they are at their best in the garden – hence spring runs from daffodils to gooseberries. Exactly when plants and crops are at their prime, however, is affected by how and where you garden, and also your local weather conditions.

The tasks featured also appear in the order they should ideally be done, although this, too, will vary for the same reasons. As a rule, judge the growing conditions outside and garden accordingly.

KEY TO SYMBOLS
🌱 **Plant type**
♠ **Height**
🍂 **Spread**
☀ **Aspect**
◉ **Soil type**
⋁ **When to plant**
◎ **When to harvest**

Spring

Signs of Spring

Spring is one of the most exciting seasons in the
garden, when all about you signs of life are poking
through the soil and filling the air. It is a time of
contrasts – a hint of the summer to come with
the threat of winter chill still lingering.

Vernal equinox

Spring is triggered by the vernal equinox, when the tilt in the Earth's orbit means the Northern Hemisphere begins to face the sun at a more direct angle. This increases the warming effect of the Sun on the Earth, dispelling the cold of winter.

Day length

Equinox means "equal night" and marks the point in the earth's orbit when the Sun is above and below the horizon for an equal time – day and night are the same length. Following the vernal equinox in mid-March, daylight hours increase and nights become shorter. This is most pronounced in northern regions, where nights can be short, staying dark for just a few hours.

Weather

The weather at this time is highly variable, and even when spring has technically begun, conditions can remain winter-like for several weeks. Hard frost and snow are common in early spring, which is often then replaced by persistent rain. Spring can also bring droughts, strong wind, and short-lived heat waves, creating challenging conditions for gardeners. The trick is to observe the weather where you are, check the forecasts, and to make the most of good spells.

Temperature

Although cold at first, spring brings improving conditions, with daytime temperatures rising from between 2–9°C to 6–15°C (36–48°F to 43–59°F) on average by the end of the season. This rise, combined with regular rainfall and increasing day length, is ideal for powering the rapid plant growth seen at this time, as seeds start to germinate, and trees, shrubs, bulbs, and perennials come into growth again.

Plant science

Spring may herald warmer weather but plants only come into growth when growing conditions are ideal. To ensure this, they have evolved their own ways to tell the weather.

SEEDS

Unlike trees, shrubs, and perennials, seeds can remain dormant for years, even centuries, and will only germinate once certain factors are met that indicate growing conditions are suitable. Although it varies between plant species, this is typically a specific combination of temperature, light, moisture, and time, but can even include exposure to extreme events, such as fire or digestion by an animal. When the conditions are right, hormones in the seed trigger it into growth. If they suddenly change, however, such as a untimely dry or cold spell, the seed will often abort germination and die.

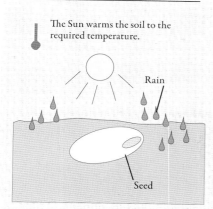

The Sun warms the soil to the required temperature.

Rain

Seed

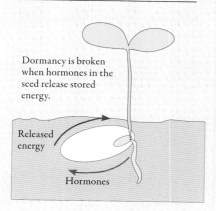

Dormancy is broken when hormones in the seed release stored energy.

Released energy

Hormones

PERENNIALS

Herbaceous perennials may appear lifeless while they are dormant but certain tissues do remain active at this time, effectively monitoring the surrounding conditions. The precise mechanism is unknown, and varies between plant species, but perennials will only emerge from dormancy when moisture, temperature, and light levels are suitable for growth. Hormones in the plant then initiate the conversion of energy-rich starch stored in the roots (as found in potatoes, for example) into sugar that is used to power the formation of new leaves and stems.

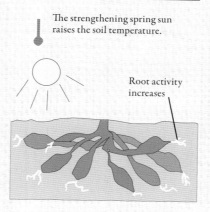

The strengthening spring sun raises the soil temperature.

Root activity increases

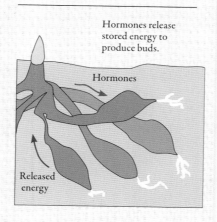

Hormones release stored energy to produce buds.

Hormones

Released energy

TREES AND SHRUBS

Trees and shrubs only emerge from dormancy once their "chilling requirement" has been met. This a period when the temperature has stayed between 1–7°C (34–45°F) for around 20 consecutive days in a row. If a warm spell occurs while the plant is dormant, its stopwatch is reset until the correct period is achieved. As temperature changes are variable, plants also monitor the changing day length using special cells, which is a more consistent measure of the changing season. Once the chilling requirement has been met, and the days are increasing in length, plants come back into growth for another year.

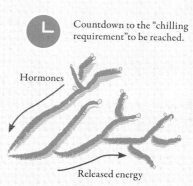

Countdown to the "chilling requirement" to be reached.

Hormones

Released energy

Energy stored in the plant is released and buds form.

The buds open into new leaves that provide energy for the plant.

Energy produced

Daffodils

The cheery trumpet blooms of daffodils, known botanically as *Narcissus*, bring swathes of colour and scent to borders, lawns, and pots throughout spring – they also make wonderful cut flowers. There are hundreds of types to choose, from miniature species to large-flowered hybrids, which vary in colour from gold to white, and even pink-tinged. Many are bi-coloured, with their trumpets and petals different shades. Once planted (*see p.258* and *p.260*), daffodils need little care. Remove spent flowers but leave the foliage to gradually die off naturally before cutting it back. To help maintain a good display, lift and divide large clumps during autumn, (*see p.261*).

AT A GLANCE
- ❧ **Plant type** Hardy bulb
- ♠ **Height** 15–50cm (6–20in)
- ☘ **Spread** 5–10cm (2–4in)
- ☀ **Aspect** Full sun or partial shade
- ◉ **Soil type** Moist but well drained

Which to choose

The traditional image of daffodils is of the golden, large-flowered varieties, such as 'Carlton' (*right*), but there are many other types to grow.

Dwarf varieties, such as 'Jack Snipe' (*above*), have a dainty appearance and look most at home in smaller sites and in containers.

White daffodils, such as 'Toto' (*above*), offer a contrast to the familiar golden forms. For greater impact, plant a mixture of shades.

Species daffodils, such as *N. bulbocodium* (*above*), have simple charm. Most are small plants, ideal for rockeries and containers.

Narcissus 'Carlton'

Camellia x *williamsii* 'Joan Trehane'

Camellias

Shrubby camellias give a spectacular show in spring,
flowering for weeks in shades of pink, white, and red.
Acid-loving, these large, dense evergreens grow well
in containers, so can be enjoyed in areas with even
alkaline soil. New plants establish best when planted
in autumn, although container-grown specimens can
be planted at any time as long as they are kept moist.
Although the plants are fully hardy, their flowers can
be damaged if they thaw too quickly after frost, so
position camellias away from direct morning
sunlight. Established plants need little routine care
or pruning, simply deadhead to keep them tidy.

AT A GLANCE
❧ **Plant type** Hardy evergreen shrub
⌂ **Height** 1–5m (3–15ft)
◣ **Spread** 1–4m (3–12ft)
☼ **Aspect** Full sun to light shade
◎ **Soil type** Acid, moist, and well drained

Choosing camellias

Spring-flowering camellias are all grown in the same way and offer a wealth of flower types – from elegantly simple to elaborate confections – in sizes and colours to suit all tastes. Height and spread varies with variety; compact camellias are ideal for large containers but larger forms are best in borders. For year-round interest, choose varieties with variegated foliage, such as *C. × williamsii* 'Golden Spangles'.

Camellia japonica 'Elegans Supreme'

C. japonica 'Tricolor'

C. reticulata 'Captain Rawes'

C. japonica 'Charlotte de Rothschild'

Containers

Compact camellias, such as *C. japonica* 'Guilio Nuccio' and 'Nuccio's Gem' are ideal for growing in containers. Choose as large a planter as you have space for, ensure it has drainage holes, and fill it with lime-free, ericaceous compost – essential for acid-loving plants. Keep camellias well watered, especially in summer when the new flower buds form, and mulch with compost each spring.

Borders

Camellias are large shrubs and perform best when planted directly in the soil, providing it is acid. Before buying camellias, check your soil using a pH testing kit, which can be bought from most garden centres. When planting, add some well-rotted garden compost to the soil, and water new plants well for the first year or two.

C. 'Lila Naff'

C. japonica 'Miss Universe'

Grow: Microgreens

Harvested as tender seedlings, microgreens are a fantastic way of enjoying delicious fresh salad leaves year-round. There are many types to try, and if you have a bright windowsill, they couldn't be easier to grow.

1 Sow the seeds into trays or pots filled with moist compost and cover with a dusting of more compost to the depth given on the seed packet. Place the tray or pot into a clear plastic bag to help conserve moisture, then place it on a warm, bright windowsill. Check daily and remove the plastic bag when seedlings start to appear.

YOU WILL NEED
* **Materials:**
Seed
Compost
* **Equipment:**
Pot or seed tray

2 Seedlings grow quickly and most types will develop their first proper pairs of leaves just days after germinating. Keep them moist at all times, although there is no need to feed them.

4 To harvest microgreens simply cut them off at the base just above the compost and discard the roots. You can then refresh the compost and sow a new batch using the same method.

Which to grow

Most leafy vegetables and herbs can be grown as microgreens, which is a good way of using up surplus seeds. For the tastiest leaves try:

- **Amaranth** (*below*), which has attractive red leaves.

- **Basil** and **coriander**, which have an aromatic flavour.

- **Beetroot**, which is colourful with a fleshy texture.

- **Lettuce**, which produces mini leaves ideal for sandwiches.

3 Microgreens are ready to harvest once they have grown two or three pairs of leaves, or are large enough to handle easily. Don't allow them to grow any larger.

Spinach 'Apollo'

Spinach

Tasty fresh spinach is a fast-growing crop that can be enjoyed for many months of the year if sown regularly. The key to sweet tender leaves is to plant spinach in rich soil that contains a lot of organic matter, and to water it frequently in dry weather. Regular watering in summer is essential, as dry spells cause plants to "bolt" – to suddenly flower – making them inedible. Sow the seed 1cm (½in) deep in rows spaced about 30cm (12in) apart; thin the seedlings to 10–15cm (4–6in) apart. Harvest the leaves regularly once they're large enough. Spinach can also be grown in pots if kept moist.

AT A GLANCE
❧ **Plant type** Annual
☀ **Aspect** Full sun or light shade
◎ **Soil type** Fertile and moist
↓ **Sow seed** Early spring – late autumn
◎ **Harvest** Late spring – winter

Growing advice

Spinach is one of the quickest and easiest crops to grow, and is ideal for smaller plots. Sow the seeds directly where the plants are to grow.

Harvesting baby leaves provides a quick crop that can even be grown in windowboxes. Sow seed and harvest the leaves after 2–3 weeks.

Spinach bolts and the leaves become tough and unpalatable if soil becomes dry. If this happens, quickly sow a new batch of seeds.

Magnolia x *soulangeana* 'Brozzonii'

Magnolias

Whether they are large and bowl-like or small and starry, the showy flowers of magnolia are a stunning sight in spring. This is a varied group of plants that ranges from compact deciduous shrubs to large evergreen trees, with varieties to suit all gardens. Although fully hardy, cold winds or frost can damage their blossom, so plant in a sheltered spot and choose a later-flowering variety if you live in a cold area. Buy the biggest container-grown plant you can afford as it will establish better, and mulch it regularly with garden compost. Keep plants well watered in summer, as this is when the flower buds develop for spring.

AT A GLANCE
❈ **Plant type** Hardy tree or shrub
❦ **Height** 3–20m (10–70ft)
◖ **Spread** 4–15m (12–50ft)
☀ **Aspect** Sun or light shade in shelter
◉ **Soil type** Moist but well drained

Which to choose

The classic magnolia, *M.* x *soulangeana* (*right*), bears pink or white flowers, and is best in larger gardens. More compact magnolias are available.

Most magnolias have pink, purple, or white blooms, making yellow-flowered 'Daphne' something special. It grows to 4m (12ft) tall.

'Black Tulip' is another compact variety that is ideal for smaller plots. Its intense purple flowers can measure up to 15cm (6in) across.

Known as the star magnolia, *M. stellata* bears masses of dainty white flowers. It is compact enough to grow in a large patio container.

Broad bean 'Aquadulce Claudia'

Broad beans

Helping to fill the "hungry gap" in mid-spring when there is little else to pick, broad beans are one of the first crops to harvest. They are also easy to grow, and maturing early means they can soon be replaced with summer crops. In mild areas, seeds can be sown from autumn to late winter into small pots to give an early crop. Choose a variety suitable for autumn sowing and protect the seedlings from cold weather with a cloche or cold frame. In other areas, wait until spring. Sow seeds into small pots under cover or directly outside, 5cm (2in) deep and spaced 25cm (10in) apart. When harvesting broad beans, pick the pods from the bottom first and work your way up.

Growing advice

Once they are established and start to grow strongly, broad beans need only minimal care, other than regular watering during dry spells.

Provide support while the plants are still small, running canes and string along the rows. Heavily laden plants can topple over.

Pinching out the growing tips when the first flowers appear helps to deter blackfly and encourages the pods to develop (*see p.188*).

AT A GLANCE
- ❧ **Plant type** Hardy annual
- ☀ **Aspect** Full sun, sheltered from wind
- ◉ **Soil type** Moist and well drained
- ⌄ **Sow seed** Mid-autumn – mid-spring
- ◎ **Harvest** Late spring – midsummer

Beetroots

Earthy and sweet tasting, beetroots are very easy to
grow, and can be harvested as baby roots a few weeks
after sowing or left to reach full size in about 90 days.
The crisp leaves can also be enjoyed as a tasty cut-and-
come-again salad crop, making this a good all-round
crop for growing in small spaces, even in containers.
Sow seed directly into the soil from mid-spring in rows
(*see pp.70–71*), and thin the seedlings to 10cm (4in)
apart as they develop. Keep the seedlings well watered
and remove any weeds that appear. Sow new batches
of seed every four weeks for a regular harvest.

AT A GLANCE
- ⚘ **Plant type** Hardy annual
- ☼ **Aspect** Full sun or light shade
- ◉ **Soil type** Fertile and well drained
- ⌄ **Sow seed** Early spring – midsummer
- ◎ **Harvest** Late spring – mid-autumn

Which to choose

There is a large range of beetroot varieties to grow, which vary in size, shape, and colour, and include unusual orange- and white-fleshed types.

'**Bulls Blood**' has firm and fleshy, deep red roots, and attractive dark red leaves that can be used to add vibrant colour to salads.

'**Chioggia Pink**' has bright red roots that when sliced open, reveal striking alternating rings of attractive pink and white flesh.

Bulbs for
Spring colour

No garden should be without bulbs, and time spent planting in autumn will be rewarded with weeks of colour in spring. Plant a wide variety in containers and beds to keep the colour coming.

1 *Anemone coronaria* In shades of mauve, red, or white, these bulbs make excellent cut flowers.
🌷 25cm (10in) ◣ 20cm (8in)

2 *Anemone blanda* Flowering in shades of blue or white, these are a cheery sight in early spring.
🌷 10cm (4in) ◣ 10cm (4in)

3 *Erythronium revolutum* Best in light shade, the pink flowers are held above marbled leaves.
🌷 30cm (12in) ◣ 15cm (6in)

4 *Puschkinia scilloides* Ideal for naturalizing or containers, it has blue or white star-like blooms.
🌷 15cm (6in) ◣ 10cm (4in)

5 *Fritillaria meleagris* With its chequerboard flowers, snake's head fritillaries should be planted *en masse* for the best effect.
🌷 30cm (12in) ◣ 10cm (4in)

6 *Scilla siberica* Suitable for planting beneath deciduous shrubs, it has bell-shaped flowers.
🌷 15cm (6in) ◣ 5cm (2in)

7 *Muscari armeniacum* Grape hyacinths quickly form natural clumps. Ideal for borders or pots.
🌷 15cm (6in) ◣ 10cm (4in)

8 *Crocus vernus* A carpet of crocuses create a spectacle in early spring. Plant in borders, rock gardens, or naturalize in grass.
🌷 10cm (4in) ◣ 5cm (2in)

9 *Hyacinthus orientalis* There is no mistaking the sweet scent of hyacinths, which flower in shades of white, pink, purple, or blue.
🌷 25cm (10in) ◣ 10cm (4in)

10 *Iris reticulata* These dwarf irises are among the earliest bulbs to emerge. Ideal for pots.
🌷 15cm (6in) ◣ 2cm (1in)

Swiss chard 'Bright Lights'

Which to grow

There is only a small range of varieties to choose, all of which are grown in the same way. The main difference is the colour and size of their stems.

'**Bright Lights**' produces glossy and brightly coloured stems in shades of yellow, red, and purple. The colour fades after cooking.

'**Lucullus**' has sturdy white stems that can be cooked like asparagus, while the leaves can be stripped and steamed like spinach.

Swiss chard

One of the earliest and latest crops to harvest, Swiss chard is grown for its large leaves and crisp stems, and is used in a similar way to spinach in the kitchen. It is a stately plant with glossy foliage and brightly coloured stems, and can even be grown alongside summer bedding. Chard likes a rich soil with lots of organic matter incorporated. Sow seed thinly in rows 2cm (¾in) deep, spaced 40cm (16in) apart. Thin the seedlings to 30cm (12in). Water them well during dry periods to prevent plants from "bolting" – suddenly flowering – and protect with fleece in winter. Pick leaves individually, the oldest ones first, leaving the plant to grow.

AT A GLANCE
- ❦ **Plant type** Hardy biennial
- ☼ **Aspect** Full sun or dappled shade
- ◉ **Soil type** Fertile and moist
- ↓ **Sow seed** Late spring – early autumn
- ◎ **Harvest** Late spring – winter

Tulips

Few garden plants offer the sheer diversity of flower shape, colour, and form as tulips. From simple, single-flowered types to the flamboyant parrot tulips, there are varieties to suit all gardens and all are very easy to grow in beds and containers. Tulips are available to buy from late summer but are best planted during late autumn (*see p.271*) to help avoid the fatal disease, *tulip fire*. When buying tulip bulbs, avoid any with signs of mould or damage. On heavy soils, add a handful of grit to the bottom of the planting holes. Once the leaves have died back after flowering, lift and store the bulbs until late autumn (*see p.188*).

AT A GLANCE
- ❧ **Plant type** Hardy bulb
- ⬆ **Height** 10–75cm (4–30in)
- ◼ **Spread** 5–10cm (2–4in)
- ☀ **Aspect** Full sun to light shade
- ◉ **Soil type** Fertile and well drained

Tulipa 'Golden Parrot'

Planting partners

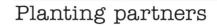

Tulip varieties range in height from dwarf to tall forms, and can be planted with many other spring-flowering plants for a colourful display.

Dwarf spring bulbs, such as muscari (*above*) look effective planted alongside tulips. Also add crocus and dwarf daffodils to provide earlier colour.

Biennial wallflowers are similar in height to many taller tulips, meaning they can support the tall blooms and provide an attractive backdrop.

Forget-me-nots are low-growing plants when young, and provide colourful ground cover and contrast beneath taller tulip varieties.

Choosing tulips

Taller tulip varieties are ideal for borders, where their graceful flowers are held above the neighbouring plants, and where they can be sheltered from strong wind and rain that can damage them. Shorter varieties are more versatile and are a good choice for the front of borders, containers, and windowboxes. Smaller-flowered species tulips, such as *T. clusiana,* are excellent for naturalizing in lawns.

'White Triumphator'

'Dyanito'

'Blue Parrot'

'Black Parrot'

'Flying Dutchman'

'Captain Fryatt'

'May Blossom'

'China Pink'

'Asta Nielsen'

'West Point'

'Greenland'

Cut flowers

Tulips are easy to grow for cutting and should be picked before the flowers are fully open. To save robbing your borders of colour, plant the bulbs in spare soil, such as in an empty vegetable bed, or in large containers. Once cut, discard the bulbs as growth the following year will be poor.

Indoor pots

For indoor displays, plant dwarf varieties into pots of compost during mid-autumn. Stand them outside in a cool, sheltered spot for at least eight weeks and regularly check the base of the pot for signs of roots. When roots show, bring the pot indoors into a cool, bright room, moving them to a warmer position once the shoots are 5cm (2in) tall. Keep them watered and they will flower within two weeks.

Patio planters

Most bulbs should be planted to a depth of three times the height of the bulb, and since tulip bulbs are quite large, they're planted deeper than many others. If planting bulbs in containers, start with the largest bulbs and plant in layers separated by compost. Bedding plants can be planted at the surface, which the bulbs will grow through.

Asparagus

Widely regarded as a delicacy, nothing beats the taste of freshly harvested, home-grown asparagus. Growing your own requires patience, however, as new plants take three years to produce their first crop. It is also a large plant that needs plenty of space, so is only suited to bigger plots. New bare-root crowns are planted in spring into well drained soil. Keep them well watered and weed-free during summer, and mulch them with garden compost each spring. Plants should also be protected from strong winds. After three years, the emerging "spears" are cut for about six weeks, after which the plants are left to grow.

AT A GLANCE
- ❦ **Plant type** Hardy perennial
- ☀ **Aspect** Full sun
- ◉ **Soil type** Fertile and well-drained
- ↓ **When to plant** Spring
- ◎ **Harvest** Late spring – early summer

Growing advice

Once established, asparagus needs little care and will crop reliably for many years. The plants are only harvested from for a few weeks each year.

Harvest the spears when 20cm (8in) tall, cutting them off 2.5cm (1in) below the soil surface. An old kitchen knife is ideal for this.

Leave plants to grow after harvesting, then cut the stems down to the soil in autumn. This period ensures a good crop next spring.

Prunus 'Kanzan'

Flowering cherries

Festooned with blossom in spring, ornamental forms of *Prunus* make excellent garden trees. There are hundreds of varieties to choose from, with their flowers ranging from white to crimson, and from dainty single florets to large double confections. Many are ideal for smaller gardens, while some also have the added bonus of beautiful autumn leaves, too. Established trees need little care, but can simply be pruned in midsummer to maintain their shape or size.

AT A GLANCE
- ❧ **Plant type** Deciduous trees
- ♠ **Height** 3–12m (10–40ft)
- ♣ **Spread** 3–12m (10–40ft)
- ☼ **Aspect** Full sun
- ◉ **Soil type** Fertile, moist, well drained

Which to choose

Double-flowered *P.* 'Kanzan' (*left*) gives a vivid show of large deep pink flowers from mid-spring. It has a broad habit, seen best in larger gardens.

Upright and compact, *P.* 'Pandora' produces masses of single pale pink blooms in early spring. It is suitable for average-sized gardens.

Weeping cherry, *P. pendula* 'Pendula Rubra' is ideal for smaller gardens. It has an elegant arching habit and flowers in late spring.

Peas

Peas never taste sweeter than when eaten within hours of picking from the garden. Easy to grow, even in containers, seed can be sown from early spring, 5cm (2in) deep and at 7.5cm (3in) intervals in rows. These are climbing plants and require the support of twiggy sticks or plastic netting – install this after sowing. Keep plants well watered and mulch around them to conserve moisture. Harvest the pods when the peas inside are swollen but tender.

Pea 'Ambassador'

Which to choose

The traditional peas are the podding varieties, which are shelled before eating. Other types include mange tout and sugar snap peas, which are grown in exactly the same way but are harvested slightly differently.

Mange tout peas are eaten "pod and all", rather than shelled. Harvest them just as the peas begin to swell inside the pods.

Sugar snap varieties are also grown for their edible pods – not the peas inside. Let the pods swell but pick before the peas develop within.

AT A GLANCE
- ❦ **Plant type** Hardy annual
- ☼ **Aspect** Full sun
- ◉ **Soil type** Fertile, moist, well drained
- ⅴ **Sow seed** Early spring – early summer
- ◎ **Harvest** Early summer – late summer

Flowers for
Spring scent

1

2

3

4

Spring is a season for heady scents, with many plants to grow that will fragrance the air on a sunny day. Some are pervasive enough to stop you in your tracks, while others require you to enjoy their charms at closer quarters.

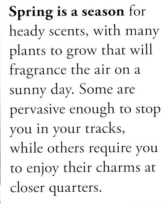

5

6

1 Osmanthus delavayi For sun or partial shade, this evergreen shrub has highly scented flowers.
🌱 4m (12ft) 🔲 4m (12ft)

2 Viola cornuta These violets have a peppery sweet scent. Plant them at the edge of a border.
🌱 15cm (6in) 🔲 10cm (4in)

3 Choisya ternata This evergreen shrub is known as Mexican orange blossom due to its sweetly scented white flowers in late spring.
🌱 2.5m (8ft) 🔲 2.5m (8ft)

4 Primula vulgaris One of the first spring flowers, the scent of primroses is best enjoyed up close.
🌱 10cm (4in) 🔲 10cm (4in)

5 Polygonatum odoratum The graceful flowers of Solomon's seal have a rich lily-like perfume.
🌱 50cm (20in) 🔲 50cm (20in)

6 Daphne x burkwoodii The scent of this evergreen shrub will fill the garden from late spring to early summer. Ideal for shade.
🌱 1.5m (5ft) 🔲 1.8m (6ft)

7 Mahonia x media This architectural evergreen shrub fills the air with its sweet fragrance from late autumn to early spring.
🌱 3m (10ft) 🔲 3m (10ft)

8 Viburnum carlesii With its pink and white blooms, this deciduous shrub has a heady aroma.
🌱 2m (6ft) 🔲 2m (6ft)

9 Corylopsis pauciflora The bell-shaped flowers of winter hazel have a delicious cowslip scent.
🌱 1.5m (5ft) 🔲 2.5m (8ft)

10 Erysimum cheiri Biennial wallflowers bring a mass of colour and scent to spring borders. They also make good cut flowers.
🌱 60cm (2ft) 🔲 30cm (1ft)

Rhododendron 'Sneezy'

Rhododendrons

A rhododendron in full flower is a spectacular sight, and is a sure sign of spring. This is a diverse group of plants, with thousands to choose from, ranging from knee-high shrubs to garden giants, and include evergreen and deciduous forms (most azaleas). They flower in a wide spectrum of colours, bearing simple trumpets to large corsage-type blooms, and many pink- or white-flowered varieties are scented. Some also have variegated foliage, giving them year-round interest. Most rhododendrons are fully hardy, although they prefer a sheltered site, while some early-flowering forms benefit from winter protection. All require acid soil, so check yours before buying. If it's alkaline, consider growing dwarf and compact forms in containers or in raised beds of lime-free soil.

AT A GLANCE
- **Plant type** Hardy shrub
- **Height** 60cm–6m (2–20ft)
- **Spread** 60cm–6m (2–20ft)
- **Aspect** Full sun or dappled shade
- **Soil type** Acid, moist, well drained

Choosing rhododendrons

Some of the best for most gardens are the compact *R. yakushimanum* and *R. williamsianum* hybrids, which are ideal for borders or containers. Taller varieties can be very dramatic but since rhododendrons only flower in spring, you may not want to dedicate so much space to them.

Rhododendron decorum

'Ilam Cream'

'Nova Zembla'

'Vanessa Pastel'

'Furnivall's Daughter'

'Odee Wright'

'Spek's Orange'

'Purple Splendour'

Planting partners

Pieris

These compact evergreen shrubs bear weeping chains or upright spikes of pink or white flowers in spring. These are followed by attractive red flame-like shoots. Pieris grows in sun or part shade, and needs rich, moist acid soil. 'Forest Flame' is widely available.

Camellias

These beautiful shrubs have glossy evergreen leaves and charming flowers that range in colour from white to dark red. Most flower in late winter or early spring, but some, such as *C. sasanqua*, flower from late autumn, and are scented, too. They need similar growing conditions to rhododendrons – they like shelter, dappled shade, and moisture in summer.

Enkianthus

Producing pendent clusters of pink or white flowers in late spring, these deciduous shrubs bloom just as rhododendrons finish flowering. They also offer further interest in autumn, as their leaves turn vibrant red. Plant them in full sun or partial shade in humus-rich, moist but well drained, acid soil.

Lettuces

This salad-leaf staple can be grown and harvested almost all year, if sown regularly and given winter protection. There are two main types to grow, open-centred loose-leaf lettuce, and tightly closed crispheads. Both can be harvested young as a cut-and-come-again crop, or as mature plants. Lettuce seed is sown 1cm (½in) deep, at 10cm (4in) intervals, in rows 30cm (12in) apart. They can also be grown in containers, which helps to protect them from slugs.

AT A GLANCE
- 🌱 **Plant type** Annual
- ☀ **Aspect** Full sun or dappled shade
- ⊛ **Soil type** Fertile and moist
- ↓ **Sow seed** Early spring – mid-autumn
- ◎ **Harvest** Late spring – mid-autumn

Growing advice

There are lots of lettuce varieties to grow, all of which are sown and raised in the same way. The main difference is how you harvest them.

Crisphead lettuce, which include 'Little Gem' (*above*), are harvested as mature heads, cut off at the base several weeks after sowing.

Loose-leaf lettuce, which include 'Lollo Rosso' (*above*), can be picked as individual leaves, leaving the plant to continue growing.

All lettuce types can be harvested as baby leaves as soon as they are large enough. Take individual leaves or harvest whole seedlings.

Radish 'Rougette'

Radishes

This succulent and peppery root crop is one
of the quickest and easiest to grow, and can
be ready to harvest in as little as five weeks
from sowing. Early crops can be started under
cover by sowing seed in pots, thinning them as
they grow, then planting them outside to reach
maturity. Maincrops are sown directly in the
soil, 2cm (¾in) deep, at 1cm (½in) intervals,
in rows spaced 10cm (4in) apart. Seedlings
should be thinned to 5cm (2in) – use the
"thinnings" as a peppery salad leaf. As they are
quick-growing and require little space, radish
are ideal for sowing in containers and between
slower-maturing crops (*see p.62*). For a regular
supply of radishes, sow seed every two weeks.

AT A GLANCE
🌺 **Plant type** Annual
☀ **Aspect** Full sun or dappled shade
⊚ **Soil type** Free-draining
↓ **Sow seed** Early spring – midsummer
◎ **Harvest** Mid-spring – late autumn

Which to grow

Radish are quick growing and should be pulled as soon as they are large enough to use. If left to grow for too long, the roots become woody.

Globe-shaped radish are perfect for salads, and are often small enough to be eaten whole. Varieties include 'Cherry Belle' (*above*).

Cylindrical radish varieties, such as 'French Breakfast 3' (*above*), are easier to handle and slice for use in salads and sandwiches.

Lilacs

Free-flowering and richly fragrant, these deciduous shrubs fill the air from late spring to early summer with sweet scent. Larger forms are a good source of cut flowers. Botanically named *Syringa*, their blooms range from white and purple, through to dark red. Lilacs thrive in most soils and tolerate air pollution, making them ideal for urban gardens. Mulch with garden compost in early spring and remove the faded flowerheads with secateurs.

Syringa vulgaris 'Masséna'

Which to choose

The common lilac, *S. vulgaris*, reaches the size of a small tree, and is best grown in larger gardens. Where space is more limited, consider smaller shrubby species.

S.* x *laciniata flowers in late spring, bearing clusters of scented purple blooms. It grows to 2 x 3m (6 x 10ft) in height and spread.

S. meyeri 'Palibin' is a compact shrub that produces small heads of pale pink flowers in late spring. It reaches 2 x 1.5m (6 x 5ft).

AT A GLANCE
- ❧ **Plant type** Deciduous shrub
- ⚘ **Height** 2–7m (6–22ft)
- ◱ **Spread** 1.5–7m (5–22ft)
- ☀ **Aspect** Full sun
- ◉ **Soil type** Fertile and well drained

S. vulgaris
'Katherine Havemeyer'

S. vulgaris
'Maud
Notcutt'

Carrot 'Mignon'

Carrots

This versatile crop is quick and easy to grow, and can be harvested as sweet and tender baby carrots a few weeks after sowing, or be left to reach full size. In addition to the familiar carrots with long orange roots, there are also those with round, purple, or white roots to try. Prepare the soil and remove any stones, which can distort the shape of the roots, and sow the seed 2cm (¾in) deep. Depending on variety, thin the seedlings to 2–12cm (¾–5in) apart. Protect plants from carrot fly (*see p.85*) and keep them well watered, as dry spells can make carrots too tough to eat. They can then be harvested once they reach your desired size.

Growing advice

Avoid handling carrot plants or splashing them with water, as this releases their aroma, which will attract root-damaging carrot fly.

In smaller gardens, or where space is limited, varieties with shorter roots, such as 'Parmex' and 'Carson' can be grown in containers.

In the vegetable patch, carrots are ideal for sowing among rows of slow-growing crops, like onions, making best use of the space.

AT A GLANCE
- ❧ **Plant type** Biennial
- ☀ **Aspect** Full sun
- ◉ **Soil type** Well drained and stoneless
- ⌄ **Sow seed** Early spring – late summer
- ◎ **Harvest** Late spring – late autumn

Gooseberries

Tart and juicy, this is one of the earliest fruits to crop. Gooseberries are delicious in crumbles, pies, fools, and jams, and they also freeze very well for use later on. New plants are best planted during autumn (*see p.274*), and can be grown naturally as bushes or trained into space-saving cordons against a wall. In smaller plots, they can also be grown in large containers filled with soil-based compost. Gooseberries are easy to grow. Prune them in summer and winter (*see p.191* and *p.302*), taking care of the sharp thorns that some varieties have. To protect the crop from birds, cover plants in spring with taut netting, secured at the base.

Which to choose

Dessert varieties are sweet enough to eat fresh from the bush, while sharp-tasting culinary types should be cooked. The fruits can be bright green, like 'Invicta' (*right*), or red, like Hinnonmäki Röd (*below*).

'Hinnonmäki Röd' (dessert)

AT A GLANCE
- ❧ **Plant type** Hardy deciduous shrub
- ♠ **Height** 1–1.5m (3–5ft)
- ◣ **Spread** 1–1.5m (3–5ft)
- ☀ **Aspect** Full sun or partial shade
- ◉ **Soil type** Moist and well drained
- ◎ **Harvest** Late spring – midsummer

Gooseberry 'Invicta' (culinary)

Jobs to do:
Spring

Around the garden:
- Protect plants from frost damage.
- Control weeds as they appear.
- Start mowing existing lawns or grow a new one from seed or turf.

On the veg patch:
- Sow vegetable seed directly outside and under cover.
- Harvest crops as they mature.

In beds and borders:
- Sow summer annuals from seed.
- Prune shrubs grown for summer flowers or winter stems.
- Plant summer-flowering bulbs.

🪏 Early spring

This is a busy time in the garden, with preparations to make before your trees, shrubs, and perennials come into full growth, and you can start planting new plants. Use these lists to prioritize what to sow, plant, and harvest, and the jobs to try to get done – weather permitting.

Essential jobs:
* Protect tender plants from frost using fleece (*see p.69*).
* Sow hardy seeds directly into the soil outside (*see pp.70–71*).
* Mulch beds, containers, and borders with compost (*see p.70*).
* Deadhead bulbs that have finished flowering (*see p.71*).
* Sow tender seeds under cover into trays and pots (*see pp.72–73*).
* Order plug plants and modules to grow on under cover.
* Prune shrubs that flower during summer (*see p.73*).
* Begin mowing lawns as they start growing again (*see p.74*).
* Chit potato tubers (*see p.75*)
* Plant summer-flowering bulbs, such as lilies (*see p.260*).

Last chance to:
* Divide perennials as their new shoots appear (*see p.261*).
* Plant new deciduous hedges, such as beech (*see p.266*).
* Finish planting new bare-root deciduous trees, shrubs, and fruit bushes (*see p.272*).
* Prune fruit trees, including apples and pears (*see p.305*).

Continue to:
* Create air holes in the surface of frozen ponds (*see p.304*).
* Treat garden timber with wood preservative (*see p.306*).
* Warm up bare soil (*see p.309*).
* Provide water and food daily for garden wildlife.

Crops to sow:
Outside: Broad beans, parsnips, peas, spinach, sprouting broccoli, and summer cabbages and cauliflowers.
Under cover: Aubergines, beetroots, Brussels sprouts, calabrese, carrots, celeriac, celery, chillies, kohl rabi, leeks, lettuces, microgreens, peppers, radishes, tomatoes, and turnips.

Crops to plant:
Broad beans, early potatoes, Jerusalem artichokes, onion and shallot sets, peas, and summer cauliflowers.

Harvest now:
Brussels sprouts, celeriac, Jerusalem artichokes, kale, leeks, microgreens, parsnips, sprouting broccoli, rhubarb, and winter cabbages and cauliflowers.

Watch out for:
* Slugs and snails – control them using pellets or use organic techniques.

Protect young plants from frost

Cover tender seedlings with fleece
at night but remove it during the day.
Weigh down the fleece at the edges but
keep it loose so plants aren't crushed.

Mulching ornamentals
and fruit trees and bushes helps to suppress emerging weeds, retain moisture, and improve soil structure and fertility. Ensure that the soil is well watered first, then spread a layer 10cm (4in) thick around your plants, keeping it from touching their stems directly. Good mulches to use include well-rotted garden compost, farmyard manure, and leaf mould.

Encourage bushy plants
by pinching out your seedlings. Once a seedling has a few pairs of full-sized leaves, remove the growing tip using your finger and thumb. This will ensure that the plant becomes bushy, with plenty of sideshoots and flower buds (*see p.91*). You can do this several times if the plant looks lanky.

Sowing hardy seeds outside

1 First dig the soil, then rake the surface thoroughly until it is fine and level. Using a dibber or the back of a trowel, make a shallow drill to the length required. Check the back of the seed packet to see how deep to make the drill.

2 Sow seeds thinly along the drill at the spacing recommended on the packet. Larger seeds can be placed more precisely. Fill in the drill with soil, and water the seeds using a can fitted with a rose.

Harvest the last of your winter crops while they are still good to eat. These include leeks, swedes, kale, parsnips, winter cabbages, celeriac, chicory, Swiss chard, Brussels sprouts, sprouting broccoli, and Jerusalem artichokes. Once the bed is clear, remove and compost any plant debris, and prepare the soil ready to sow and plant summer crops.

More jobs to do

Plants raised under cover need maximum light in order to grow strongly. Use a hose to wash algae, moss, and dirt from greenhouse and conservatory glass, and clean inside and out thoroughly with detergent.

While their stems are bare, this is the ideal time to tackle overgrown deciduous climbers and wall shrubs, such as honeysuckle. Prune the oldest stems to the base, thin congested growth, and shorten long shoots.

3 Seedlings will emerge after a week or two, depending on type, and should be kept well watered as they develop. Remove any weeds that appear at this time to prevent them competing with your plants.

4 As the seedlings grow, carefully thin them out so they aren't overcrowded and have room to develop properly. Also keep them well watered and weed-free. Thin them repeatedly as required.

Deadheading bulbs not only keeps your display looking good but ensures that energy goes back into the bulb for next year. Pinch off spent flowers now but leave the foliage to die back naturally (*see p.188*).

Netting brassica plants protects them from damaging pigeons that strip the leaves from newly planted cabbage, kale, cauliflower, and broccoli. To protect them fully, build a simple cage of bamboo canes and cover with netting or insect-proof mesh as soon as you have planted them out. Pin the netting into the soil.

Sowing tender seed indoors

1 Fill a tray with good quality, sieved seed compost and firm it down gently. Water it well using a watering can with a fine rose fitted and allow to drain. The compost should be moist to touch.

Supporting taller perennials is easiest to do now while the new shoots are emerging, and enables the plants to grow through the support, hiding it. Simple frames made from garden canes and string are effective, and can be easily adapted for tall or spreading plants.

Removing lawn weeds now will prevent them establishing, when they will be harder to control. Remove larger ones by hand or use lawn weedkiller. You can also apply high-nitrogen lawn feed to promote strong, weed-suppressing growth.

2 Sow the seeds thinly on the surface of the compost, following the spacing instructions on the packet. Larger seeds can be spaced out individually; smaller ones are best lightly sprinkled.

3 Cover the seeds with a thin layer of compost to the depth given on the seed packet. Don't be tempted to cover them too thickly as this may hinder them coming up. Label the tray so you know which seeds it contains.

4 Place the tray in a warm propagator, on a bright windowsill, or in a greenhouse, until the seeds germinate in about 2–3 weeks. Keep the compost moist at all times.

Onions and shallots

can both be grown from "sets" (immature bulbs) now, for harvesting from midsummer to autumn. Prepare the soil and plant the sets individually in rows, so that their tips are just poking slightly out of the soil. To prevent birds pulling them up, cover the sets with fleece or netting while they take root.

Time to prune Many shrubs can be pruned now to promote flowers and growth.

Deciduous shrubs that

flower from midsummer onwards, such as lavatera, are pruned now to maintain their shape and size, and to encourage flowering. Cut last year's flowered stems to within one or two buds of the older, woody framework. Water well and mulch afterwards.

Pot up seedlings raised under cover regularly to ensure continued growth. Look under their pots every few weeks, and if roots are visible, it's time to repot them into a container about an inch wider. Ease the plant from its current pot, trying not to disturb the roots, plant into the larger pot, and water it well.

Install support for climbing peas and beans before you sow or plant, as it will be tricky to do afterwards. Bamboo canes are ideal for tall climbing beans, and can be arranged in wigwams or rows. Peas are lower growing, and can be supported by netting, canes, or trellis.

Moving existing evergreen shrubs can be done now during mild spells. Water the plant the day before and prepare a suitable new hole. Working all around the plant, dig out the entire rootball, leaving it as intact as possible. Replant immediately and keep it well watered.

Start mowing the lawn on dry days once the grass shows signs of new growth. The first cut each season should just be a gentle trim – set the blades around 5mm (¼in) higher than your normal cut. Don't mow if the lawn is very wet. Trimming the edges will ensure it looks neat.

Planting early potatoes

1 Before planting seed potatoes, keep them in a cool, light spot indoors for 4–6 weeks until they produce shoots around 2cm (1in) long. This is called "chitting".

2 Dig a narrow trench, around 12cm (5in) deep, where you plan to grow your potatoes and spread well-rotted garden compost or fertilizer in the bottom.

3 Carefully put the "chitted" potatoes into the trench with the shoots pointing upwards. Space them about 30–75cm (12–30in) apart, depending on the variety.

4 Water the base of the trench thoroughly and cover the potatoes over with soil. Shoots will appear in 2–3 weeks. These will need protection from slug damage.

Mid-spring

As the weather warms up, plants start to grow rapidly now, making this a good time to sow and plant out, but it also means you need to spend time supporting and tying in new plant growth. Weeds will also be growing quickly now, so keep on top of them before they establish.

Essential jobs:
* Start hardening off plants raised under cover (*see p.77*).
* Plant new pond plants (*see p.77*).
* Grow new lawns from turf or seed (*see pp.78–79 and p.81*).
* Tie in climbers and wall shrubs as they grow (*see p.79*).
* Feed fruit trees and bushes with high potash fertilizer.
* Plant new evergreen trees, shrubs, and conifers (*see p.80*).
* Tidy up borders before plants are in full growth (*see p.80*).
* Prune frost-damaged growth from evergreens (*see p.80*).
* Remove winter bedding plants as they finish flowering.
* Mulch strawberry plants with clean, fresh straw (*see p.80*).

Last chance to:
* Divide overgrown clumps of perennials (*see p.261*).
* Buy module and plug plants to grow on under cover.

Continue to:
* Protect young and tender plants from frosts (*see p.69*).
* Weed the garden regularly.
* Sow seeds (*see pp.70–73*).
* Deadhead spring bulbs (*see p.71*).
* Support growing plants (*see p.72*).
* Mow the lawn regularly at your normal cutting height.
* Pot up growing seedlings raised under cover (*see p.74*).
* Plant out early and maincrop potatoes (*see p.75*).

Crops to sow:
Outside: Beetroots, broad beans, Brussels sprouts, carrots, kale, kohl rabi, leeks, lettuces, parsnips, peas, radishes, spinach, sprouting broccoli, summer cabbages and cauliflowers, and turnips.
Under cover: Aubergines, calabrese, French and runner beans, celeriac, celery, chillies, courgettes, cucumbers, Florence fennel, peppers, pumpkins, squashes, sweetcorn, tomatoes, and turnips.

Crops to plant:
Asparagus, early and maincrop potatoes, globe and Jerusalem artichokes, kohl rabi, lettuces, onion and shallot sets, peas, spinach, and summer cabbages and cauliflowers.

Harvest now:
Kale, leeks, radish, rhubarb, spring cabbages, sprouting broccoli, parsnips, and winter cauliflowers.

Watch out for:
* Aphids – treat with pesticide or use organic techniques.

Hardening off plants raised under cover acclimatizes them to life growing outdoors. Over a period of two to three weeks, stand plants outside during the day but bring them in at night. If you have a cold frame, place them inside, only closing the lid at night. After this period you can then leave your hardened-off plants outside and uncovered.

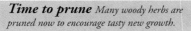

Time to prune *Many woody herbs are pruned now to encourage tasty new growth.*

Shrubby herbs, such as lavender and sage, can be lightly pruned. Remove the soft growth produced during last year, cutting back to new buds emerging on the older, woodier stems. Thin out weaker shoots and maintain a balanced shape. To prune rosemary, cut any weak stems back to strong, healthy new buds.

Planting new pond plants

1 Sit the new plant in an aquatic mesh basket (*above*) of an appropriate size – the planting depth should be same as in the original container. If it's a tall plant, such as a reed or rush, place some rocks or stones at the bottom to prevent it from blowing over. Loosen the rootball gently.

2 Fill the basket with aquatic compost that feeds the plant without the nutrients leaching into the pond water. Don't use nutrient-rich potting compost as it encourages algae that will turn the water green. Fill the basket to 5cm (2in) of the rim and firm the plant in.

3 Mulch around the plant with a 2cm (1in) layer of gravel to prevent fish from stirring up the compost. This will also help weigh down the pot in the water and make it more stable. Water the plant well or plunge it into a bucket of pond water so that the compost is saturated.

4 Gently lower the plant to its final position in the pond. Different types of plant need to be planted at specific depths, so check the planting instructions for each one. If you need to raise the pot in the water to achieve the correct depth, place it on some bricks or smooth stones.

Check compost heaps and bins, and if the material inside is dark, crumbly, and sweet smelling, it's ready to start using in the garden. Well-rotted garden compost helps to improve soil structure, moisture-retention, and ferility. Use it as a mulch (*see p.70*) or dig it into the soil when planting.

Buy bedding plants while garden centres have the best choice, and keep them in a frost-free greenhouse or cold frame for now. If you can't keep them under cover, wait until frosts are less severe before buying plants, and protect them at night using garden fleece.

Creating a new lawn using turf

1 Before laying turf, ensure the soil is flat, firm, and well-drained. Fork over the area and remove stones and weeds, then rake it level. Firm the surface by treading it over.

2 Choose turf suited to your needs, such as one that is hard-wearing. Roll out the first turf using a long plank as a straight edge, then roll out the rest, making sure the ends are staggered. Kneel on the plank, not the grass.

Earthing up potatoes

helps to support their stems, prevents the tubers from turning green by blocking sunlight, and encourages a larger crop. Starting once the new shoots have reached 20cm (8in) tall, regularly cover the base of the stems with soil all around until you have created a ridge 25cm (10in) high.

Tying in climbers and wall-trained plants

as they produce new growth encourages them to cover the surface neatly, and means they are easier to prune. Tie new shoots to their supports once they reach 10–15cm (4–6in) long, tying them in again regularly as they grow. Leave the ties loose enough for the stems to thicken.

Planting crops under cover

1 Growing bags are ideal for growing crops under cover. They require regular watering, so to help retain moisture, make as small a planting hole as possible. Use a small plant pot as a cutting guide.

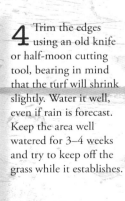

3 Butt up all the edges closely – you can overlap them a little and then push them down well. Fill in gaps between the turves by brushing compost into them. Be generous with turf around the edges so it can be shaped easily.

4 Trim the edges using an old knife or half-moon cutting tool, bearing in mind that the turf will shrink slightly. Water it well, even if rain is forecast. Keep the area well watered for 3–4 weeks and try to keep off the grass while it establishes.

2 Before planting, make drainage holes in the base and loosen the compost to break up large lumps. After planting, water your plants in well and provide supports as required.

Tidying borders while there is still space between plants is much easier than when they are in full growth. Hoe to remove weeds, cut back spent growth, and clear away all plant debris. This will also help to control many plant diseases.

Planting evergreens is best done during spring. When planted in autumn, they are prone to damage caused by cold winter winds. Dig a generous planting hole and tease out the plant's roots. Position the plant, backfill with soil, and water it in well. Water regularly during summer.

Remove frost-damaged growth from shrubs, especially evergreens, once the risk of hard frosts has passed. Prune damaged stems back to a healthy bud and pick off blackened leaves. To help the plant recover, mulch or apply fertilizer to promote healthy new growth.

Mulch around strawberry plants to keep the developing fruits off the soil. Traditionally straw was used – hence the name – but you could also use plastic strawberry mats. Straw allows good airflow around the fruits, which deters mould, while plastic mats can be reused.

Sow a new lawn

1 Prepare the area by digging the soil thoroughly to break up any lumps and remove any larger stones. Then, rake the surface well to a fine crumb and level it off. If resowing an existing lawn, remove the turf first.

2 Use garden canes to mark the area into 1m (3ft) squares. Weigh out as much seed as you need to sow in each square, and spread it evenly. The recommended sowing rate should be stated on the back of the packet.

3 Lightly rake the seed into the soil surface and water it in well using a can with a rose fitted (*see above*). The seed will germinate in a few days and should be watered regularly. Avoid walking on the lawn until established.

Time to prune *Many plants need pruning now to encourage flowering and healthy growth.*

Spring-flowering clematis, such as *C. alpina*, *C. montana*, *C. armandii*, and *C. cirrhosa* can be lightly pruned after flowering, once the last frost has passed. Remove dead and damaged stems, and trim to fit the available space. Tie in new shoots to their supports using string.

Shrubs grown for foliage are pruned before growth starts but after the frosts have passed. For the best leaves, all stems can be pruned to the base, which may result in no flowers. As a compromise, cut some stems to the base, leaving the rest to flower later in the season.

Spring-flowering shrubs, such as flowering currants, weigela, and forsythia, flower on last year's growth. When the plant has finished flowering, prune these woody stems down to just above the fresh green growth below. Leave new shoots that haven't flowered, as these will bloom next spring.

Shrubs with winter stems, such as dogwoods and willow, should be cut back hard before their new leaves appear. Remove all growth, cutting it back to within two or three buds of the base of the plant. Although drastic, this promotes strong healthy summer growth and a good display of coloured stems next winter.

Late spring

The risk of frosts will soon be over, allowing you to harden off and plant out tender crops and ornamentals raised under cover. As the soil starts to warm, seeds sown directly will germinate quickly but more pests are also active now. Take precautions and check plants for signs of early damage.

Essential jobs:

✴ Start trimming evergreens to keep them neat (*see p.83*).
✴ Plant out tender vegetables raised under cover (*see p.84*).
✴ Take softwood cuttings from shrubby plants (*see p.84*).
✴ Ventilate plants growing under cover (*see p.85*).
✴ Install insect-proof netting over vegetable crops (*see p.85*).
✴ Lift and divide congested spring bulbs (*see p.261*).
✴ Tidy up spring-flowering perennials, such as hellebores.
✴ Thin out developing gooseberries to encourage larger berries.
✴ Hang codling moth traps in the branches of your fruit trees to avoid maggoty apples and pears.

Last chance to:

✴ Sow tender vegetables from seed under cover (*see pp.72–73*).
✴ Clean garden furniture.

Continue to:

✴ Sow hardy quick-growing crops directly in the soil (*see pp.70–71*).
✴ Stake perennial plants and taller bulbs as they grow (*see p.72*).
✴ Earth up potatoes (*see p.79*).
✴ Tie in climbers and wall shrubs as they grow (*see p.79*).
✴ Water crops and young plants regularly during dry spells.
✴ Weed beds and borders.
✴ Mow the lawn and trim the edges, removing the clippings.

Watch out for:

✴ Lily beetle on lilies and fritillaries – squash them and their larvae on sight.

Crops to sow:

Under cover: Courgettes, cucumbers, French and runner beans, pumpkins, squashes, and sweetcorn.

Outside: Beetroots, Brussels sprouts, calabrese, carrots, Florence fennel, kale, kohl rabi, leeks, lettuces, parsnips, peas, radishes, spinach, summer cabbages, sprouting broccoli, swede, Swiss chard, turnips, and winter cabbages and cauliflowers.

Crops to plant:

Aubergines, Brussels sprouts, celeriac, celery, chillies, courgettes, cucumbers, early and maincrop potatoes, Florence fennel, globe and Jerusalem artichokes, kohl rabi, leeks, onion and shallot sets, peppers, pumpkins, squashes, strawberries, sprouting broccoli, summer cabbages and cauliflowers, and tomatoes.

Harvest now:

Asparagus, beetroots, broad beans, carrots, gooseberries, lettuces, peas, radishes, rhubarb, spinach, spring cabbages, strawberries, Swiss chard, and winter cauliflowers.

Pruning evergreens

Most evergreens need only minor pruning and are trimmed to shape as new growth appears. Any dead or diseased material should be removed. Prune spring-flowering shrubs after flowering has finished.

Grow plants from softwood cuttings

1 This type of cutting uses the new, soft shoots and can be used to grow most shrubby plants, including herbs. Early in the day, cut off pieces of non-flowering new growth, cutting just above a bud or leaf on the parent plant.

2 Using a sharp knife, cut the stem just below a leaf, making a cutting that's 5–10cm (2–4in) long. Trim the leaves from the bottom half and pinch out the soft tip. Dip the base of the stem into rooting powder to help encourage roots to form.

Planting out tender crops, such as courgettes, tomatoes, squashes, pumpkins, chillies, French and runner beans, sweetcorn, and outdoor cucumbers, that were raised under cover can begin once the risk of frost has passed. Be sure to harden them off fully first (*see p.77*), before planting them into containers or well prepared soil. Protect all new plantings against slug damage.

3 In a pot, insert the cuttings into moist, gritty compost. Water them again and cover the pot with a clear plastic bag to retain moisture. Place in a light spot under cover and the cuttings will root in 4–6 weeks.

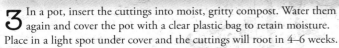

Covering crops with fine netting is an effective way to protect them from carrot fly larvae, which burrow into the roots of carrots, parsnips, parsley, Florence fennel, celery, and celeriac, stunting their growth and ruining the harvest. Secure the netting at soil level or bury it slightly to prevent the adult flies crawling beneath it.

Frost protection material can be removed from tender plants once the risk of frost has passed. Keep it handy, in case a late frost is forecast and you need to protect any plants temporarily. Brush the material clean and store it away until autumn.

Strawberry plants produce baby plantlets on long stems called "runners", which can be used in summer to grow new replacements (*see p.190*). Unless you want new plants, however, they are best removed now to prevent the plants wasting energy that would otherwise be used to produce fruit. Simply pinch them off with your fingers or cut the stems with scissors.

Ventilate greenhouses, cloches, and cold frames on warm days to prevent the plants inside overheating and drying out. High temperatures now also encourage soft growth, which is easily damaged by cold conditions. Close the doors, vents, and lids at night, especially if low temperatures are forecast.

Summer

Signs of Summer

This is the most colourful season in the garden, with plants flowering and growing strongly, crops ready to harvest, and borders at their peak. The long, warm, and sunny days allow more opportunities to spend time in the garden, although dry spells mean regular watering.

Summer solstice

In the Northern Hemisphere the summer solstice occurs on or around 21ˢᵗ June. This is the point at which the Earth is tilted most closely towards the Sun on its annual orbital path. This results in warmer temperatures and increased light levels. If planning a new garden now, bear in mind that an area sunny in high summer may be shady at other times.

Day length

The summer solstice marks the longest day, as measured in daylight hours – days around this time typically offer 16 hours of light. However, as the Earth continues on its orbit, the days start getting shorter from midsummer. The solstice is also an important point for plants described as "short day plants" (*see p.91*), such as chrysanthemums and sedums, which will soon come into flower.

Weather

There's no such thing as a typical summer's day in the UK, where the weather can change quickly from warm and dry to cool and wet. Extremes of temperature, rainfall, and sunshine are not uncommon. Generally, it's wetter the farther north and west you go, and drier in the south and east. June is the sunniest month. It rains around one day in three, and the sun shines for an average of around 5½ hours each day. Our changeable climate makes it possible to grow a wide range of plants but it can be frustrating – the trick is to grow a variety of plants that enjoy different weather conditions.

Temperature

The average maximum temperature for the UK in summer is 18°C (65°F) but can reach over 30°C (86°F) for short periods. Temperatures are generally warmer in the south of England than in northern England and Scotland. July is typically the warmest month, although not the sunniest. Daytime temperatures can remain high even towards the end of the season, although nights become cooler.

Plant
science

Summer is the peak season for most plants
to flower and produce new growth. This is
when gardens are at their best and there's
a lot of science that makes it happen.

ANNUALS

Most summer annuals originate from habitats where events such as fire, flood, or drought are common, or where moisture or nutrition are short-lived. As their aim in life is to ensure the survival of their species, annuals have rapid lifecycles, and often flower and produce their first seeds within weeks of germinating. With seeds produced, their mission is complete, and annuals then start to die, meaning a brief display in the garden. Removing spent flowers (deadheading) before any seeds are produced forces plants to flower again to complete their mission.

Annuals flower and set seed quickly, and once enough are produced, the plants die.

Removing spent flowers before they produce seeds forces the plant to flower again.

PERENNIALS

Summer perennials will be coming into flower, and like many types of plant, this is influenced by day and night length. In a response known as "photoperiodism", many plants only come into flower once they have experienced a certain number of daylight hours relative to night. Flowering occurs when a trigger point is met, which depends on the species. Some flower before the summer solstice when days are getting longer, and are referred to as "long day" plants, while "short day" plants flower as the days become shorter after the solstice.

 Special proteins in plants react to changes in day and night length.

Plants flower when the right balance of day and night time has been met.

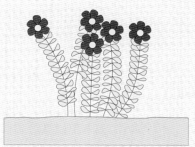

SHRUBS

Growth in all types of plant is controlled by a hormone called "auxin", which is concentrated in the main uppermost growing tips. Its role is to promote growth in the main tips and to suppress it in lower sideshoots. This is known as "apical dominance" and ensures that plants reach vertically towards the best light, which is essential for growth. Pruning plants or pinching out their main tips transfers the dominant effect to buds lower down, which then grow. The result for the gardener is shorter, bushier plants, with more flowering shoots.

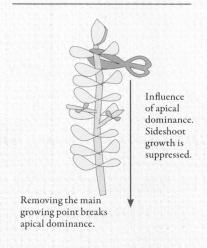

Influence of apical dominance. Sideshoot growth is suppressed.

Removing the main growing point breaks apical dominance.

On pruned plants, the uppermost sideshoots on each stem start growing.

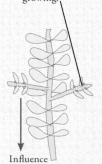

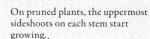

Influence of apical dominance.

If pruned, sideshoots also lose their dominance, causing them to bush out.

Allium giganteum

Alliums

With their elegant, lollipop-like blooms, opening in shades of white, yellow, pink, and purple, alliums are a distinctive sight in early summer. Later, if they are left to dry, the spent flowerheads can give interest during autumn. Alliums are ideal for beds and containers, and are best planted in early autumn (*see p.260*). The leaves die back as the blooms appear, and after flowering, the bulbs become dormant until spring.

Which to choose

The boldest alliums are those with large flowers and lofty 1m (3ft) stem, such as *A. giganteum* (*see right*), but shorter types can be just as colourful in the garden.

Dwarf species, such as the yellow-flowered *A. flavum* (*above*), are ideal for containers and rockeries. They grow to as little as 10cm (4in) tall.

Mid-height species, such as pale blue-flowered *A. caeruleum* (*above*), reach 60cm (24in) tall, and are ideal for the fronts of mixed borders.

AT A GLANCE
❦**Plant type** Hardy bulb
🌢 **Height** 10–100cm (4–39in)
🌢 **Spread** 5–20cm (2–8in)
☼ **Aspect** Full sun or light shade
◎ **Soil type** Moist but well drained

Delphinium 'Tiddles'

Delphiniums

With their elegant, flower-packed spires of colour, delphiniums are true stars of the cottage garden and herbaceous border. There are many varieties to choose, ranging from the familiar blues, to white, mauve, and pink. These are tall plants, so position them at the back of the border, and stake them early to hold them upright. Dig in garden compost when planting, mulch afterwards, and feed regularly for the best display. Cutting plants back hard after flowering often encourages a second flush of flowers. Delphiniums are prone to slugs, so take steps to control them.

AT A GLANCE
- ❦ **Plant type** Hardy perennial
- ⚘ **Height** 1.5–2m (5–6ft)
- ◭ **Spread** 60–90cm (2–3ft)
- ☀ **Aspect** Full sun
- ◎ **Soil type** Fertile and well drained

Planting partners

Delphinium flowers can be short-lived, so plant other perennials with upright flower spikes to give borders vertical emphasis and drama.

Foxgloves, *Digitalis purpurea*, flower slightly earlier than delphiniums in sun or light shade.

Monkshood, *Aconitum carmichaelii*, flowers in autumn, adding colour to shady borders.

Foxtail lily, *Eremurus stenophyllus*, flowers at the same time as delphiniums, and is a good choice to grow alongside them in full sun.

Early potatoes

Homegrown potatoes are such a treat that digging them up feels like finding buried treasure. Being harvested in early summer, they leave ample time to grow later crops, making them suitable for even small plots. The plants are started as "seed" potatoes (*see p.75*) and are easy to grow. Keep them well watered, and "earth up" regularly (*see p.79*). Harvest them when the plants flower, carefully digging around the plant with a fork.

Container growing

Early potatoes happily grow in containers, and even in large sacks. A bucket-sized pot is ideal for one plant.

AT A GLANCE
- ✹ **Plant type** Annual tuber
- ☀ **Aspect** Full sun
- ◉ **Soil type** Fertile and well drained
- ⋎ **Plant** Early spring – mid-spring
- ◎ **Harvest** Early summer – midsummer

Geranium 'Nimbus'

Border geraniums

Also known as cranesbills, this diverse group of perennials is incredibly versatile in the garden, being free-flowering and able to cope with a wide variety of planting conditions. They come in a varied range of colours and sizes, fit with any planting style, and are ideal at the front or middle of a border, or as ground cover. Many are evergreen and some have interesting autumn foliage. Geraniums grow well in most soils and need little care. Deadheading will promote a longer flowering season, and if clumps look tatty in midsummer, cut them back hard to encourage fresh new foliage, and sometimes more flowers.

AT A GLANCE
❧ **Plant type** Hardy perennial
⬥ **Height** 50–100cm (20–39in)
◣ **Spread** 50–90cm (20–36in)
☀ **Aspect** Full sun or partial-shade
◉ **Soil type** Any

Which to choose

To been seen at their best in the border, choose those species and hybrids, including 'Nimbus' (*left*), that grow to over 50cm (20in) in height.

G. pratense has dainty saucer-shaped flowers in shades of white, purple, pink, and blue. Varieties include 'Mrs Kendall Clark' (*above*).

G. x oxonianum is a vigorous perennial with a clump-forming habit. There are many varieties to choose with pink or red flowers.

G. sylvaticum flowers in early summer, bearing blue, white, pink, or purple flowers above lobed foliage. It is clump-forming.

Plant:
Hanging baskets

Hanging baskets add instant colour to the garden, and raise flowers to eye level where they can be easily enjoyed. They offer a chance to be creative and to try new planting combinations.

YOU WILL NEED
* **Materials:**
Hanging basket and liner
Plastic sheeting
Multipurpose compost
Slow-release fertilizer
Water-retaining gel crystals
Bedding plants

1 If using an open wire basket (*as above*), insert a fibre liner and place a piece of polythene on the inside to help retain moisture. This is not necessary for baskets with solid sides.

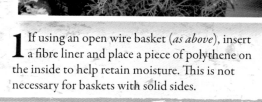

2 Fill the basket with multipurpose compost to within 5cm (2in) of the rim. Mix in some slow-release fertilizer and water-retaining gel crystals.

4 Add trailing and bushy plants around the central one, spacing them as evenly as possible. Cascading plants can also be threaded through the side of the basket. Use a sharp knife to make small slits in the liner and plastic.

5 Once all the plants are in place, carefully fill around them with more compost and firm them in. Ensure the level of the compost is 2.5cm (1in) below the rim of the basket to make watering easier.

3 Position the tallest or most upright plant in the centre of the basket, ensuring there is an even amount of space all round it for the other plants. To help the plants establish, tease their roots away from the rootball before planting.

6 Water the basket well and leave it to stand. If the compost settles and gaps appear between the plants, carefully add some more. Hang the basket in sheltered position away from strong winds.

Strawberry 'Elsanta'
(summer-fruiting)

Strawberries

An irresistible taste of summer, these are easy
fruits to grow. Just choose a sunny spot with
fertile, well-drained soil, and plant them about
30cm (12in) apart. They also grow very well in
containers and baskets, where their white or
pink flowers are as eye-catching as the fruits.
Varieties are divided into two main types
depending on when they crop (*see below*), and
it's worth planting both for the best harvest.
Replace tired old plants every two years.

Which to choose

Summer-fruiting varieties crop heavily from early- to midsummer, while
"perpetual" types produce a smaller crop from early summer to autumn.

Alpine strawberries are an alternative to garden varieties, and fruit
freely throughout summer, bearing very sweet and flavoursome
miniature berries. They are ideal for growing in patio containers.

AT A GLANCE
- ❧ **Plant type** Hardy perennial
- ☀ **Aspect** Full sun
- ☺ **Soil type** Fertile, moist, well drained
- ↓ **When to plant** Anytime if pot grown
- ◎ **Harvest** Early summer – autumn

Clematis 'Victoria'
(Group 3)

Summer clematis

Clothing fences and pergolas in colour, summer-flowering clematis are categorized according to when they flower and how they're pruned (*see p.197* and *p.309*). Group 2 consists of large-flowered hybrids that bloom in early summer, and often give a second flush later in the season. Giving two splashes of colour, they are ideal for plots where space is at a premium – there are also compact varieties, suitable for containers. Group 3 clematis have smaller blooms borne in a single flush from mid- to late summer. It is a varied group, and includes varieties that are also grown for their autumn seedheads. Plant all clematis deeply and keep their roots cool, shaded by nearby plants or with a large stone on the soil surface. Keep them well watered in summer, and mulch each spring for the best display.

AT A GLANCE
❧ **Plant type** Hardy climber
⚘ **Height** 2–4m (6–12ft)
◪ **Spread** 1–1.5m (3–5ft)
☀ **Aspect** Full sun or part shade
◉ **Soil type** Fertile, moist, and cool

Which to choose

As all clematis enjoy the same conditions, consider planting varieties from groups 2 and 3 to enjoy the longest season of colour possible.

Flowering from midsummer, *C. tangutica* (group 3) produces dainty lantern-like blooms, followed by autumn seedheads.

Group 2 variety, 'Bee's Jubilee', bears pink and white blooms up to 20cm (8in) across. Flowers in the second flush may be smaller.

Perennial
Kitchen herbs

1

2

Perennial herbs make an attractive addition to borders and containers, and provide an ever-ready supply of flavoursome leaves and shoots for the kitchen. Most are of Mediterranean origin, so prefer a sunny position and well drained soil. All are easy to grow.

3

4

5

1 Marjoram This compact herb has aromatic leaves and pretty pink flowers loved by butterflies.
✿ 45cm (18in) ◣ 30cm (12in)

2 Camomile Its scented foliage and daisy-like flowers can be dried and made into a soothing tea.
✿ 10cm (4in) ◣ 30cm (12in)

3 Rosemary This evergreen shrub has aromatic leaves and small, blue or white flowers in spring. The leaves can be used fresh or dried.
✿ 1.5m (5ft) ◣ 1m (3ft)

4 Bay This large evergreen shrub is suitable for borders or pots. The tasty leaves can be harvested all year, as required, and can be dried.
✿ 10m (30ft) ◣ 10m (30ft)

5 Mint There are many varieties of mint, each with a distinctive flavour, such as chocolate or apple. It can spread, so grow it in a pot.
✿ 60cm (2ft) ◣ 1.5m (5ft)

6 Thyme This low-growing evergreen shrub has aromatic leaves used in savoury dishes.
✿ 30cm (12in) ◣ 40cm (16in)

7 Sage This evergreen shrub has grey, purple, or variegated leaves, and small pink flowers. Pick the leaves and shoots in summer.
✿ 1m (3ft) ◣ 1m (3ft)

8 Chives Grown for its mild, oniony flavour, its pink, globe-shaped flowers are also edible.
✿ 50cm (20in) ◣ 10cm (4in)

9 Lemon balm Its attractive nettle-like, lemon-scented leaves are used to make a calming tea.
✿ 1m (3ft) ◣ 60cm (2ft)

10 Fennel This tall, feathery plant is grown for its leaves and seeds, which taste of aniseed.
✿ 2m (6ft) ◣ 60cm (2ft)

Turnip 'Atlantic'

Turnips

An ideal vegetable for small spaces, these tasty roots can be eaten young or mature, while the mustard-flavoured tops can be harvested like spring greens, giving two crops in one. Sow seed where they are to grow – including in containers – 1cm (½in) deep and thin them to 15–23cm (6–9in) apart, depending on variety. Keep them well watered during dry spells to prevent the roots becoming tough, and sow new batches of seed every 2–3 weeks.

Growing advice

Turnip varieties vary from purple- to white-skinned, with rounded or flattened roots. Some mature faster, but all are grown in the same way.

Turnips are harvested 30–65 days after sowing. To enjoy them raw as baby roots, pull them once they reach the size of a golf ball; for mature roots to eat cooked, wait until they are tennis ball-sized.

AT A GLANCE
- ❦ **Plant type** Biennial
- ☼ **Aspect** Full sun
- ◉ **Soil type** Fertile and well drained
- ⌄ **Sow seed** Early spring – late summer
- ◎ **Harvest** Early summer – late autumn

Cherry 'Nabella'
(acid)

Cherries

A delicious summer treat, fresh cherries are
expensive to buy but are now much easier to
grow at home. Modern self-fertile varieties
mean you only need one tree to produce a
crop, unlike most apples, while dwarfing
rootstocks 'Colt', 'Tabel', and 'Gisela 5' limit
their growth, making them suitable for most
gardens. The smallest forms can even be grown
in large patio containers if kept well watered.
There are two types to grow. "Sweet cherries"
can be enjoyed fresh from the tree, while sour
"acid cherries" must be cooked with plenty
of sugar. Once planted, cherries need little
routine care. Mulch trees in spring with garden
compost, protect the fruit from birds using
nets, and prune them lightly in summer to
maintain their shape (*see p.197*).

AT A GLANCE
- ❧ **Plant type** Deciduous tree
- ☗ **Height** 3–8m (10–25ft)
- ☙ **Spread** 3–6m (10–20ft)
- ☀ **Aspect** Full sun – shade (acid types)
- ⊚ **Soil type** Fertile and well drained
- ◎ **Harvest** Early summer – early autumn

Which to choose

Deciding between sweet and acid cherries is a matter of preference but seek advice on the best dwarfing rootstock to meet your requirements.

Sweet cherries include self-fertile varieties 'Stella', 'Lapins', and 'Sweetheart' (*above*), which fruit from midsummer onwards.

Acid cherries are all self-fertile and will grow in shade. Varieties include 'Morello' (*above*) and 'Nabella' (*left*), which fruit in late summer.

Bedding plants for
Summer colour

Bedding plants provide long-lasting colour in summer pots, windowboxes, and hanging baskets. You can also use them in bedding displays or to plug gaps in the borders. There is a large range to choose from, which can be grown from seed or bought as young plants in spring. Most require a sunny spot. For the best display, keep them deadheaded, and water and feed them regularly.

1 Petunias These can be low and bushy or trailing, and flower in a huge range of colours. Height and spread depends on type.

2 Ageratum This annual has fluffy blooms in shades of pink or blue, which are loved by bees.
♠ 20cm (8in) ⬧ 25cm (10in)

3 Marguerites These shrubby perennials have daisy-like blooms in a range of colours. They can be overwintered under cover.
♠ 30cm (12in) ⬧ 40cm (16in)

4 Gazanias Best in full sun, its brightly coloured, daisy-like flowers close up in cloudy spells.
♠ 25cm (10in) ⬧ 25cm (10in)

5 Lobelia Smothered in white, pink, or blue flowers, this annual can be bushy or trailing. Height and spread depends on type.

6 Tagetes These free-flowering annuals bloom all summer, forming neat mounds of colour.
♠ 25cm (10in) ⬧ 25cm (10in)

7 Swan river daisies Low and bushy, this annual flowers freely in shades of white, pink, or blue.
♠ 25cm (10in) ⬧ 25cm (10in)

8 Snapdragons Cottage garden favourites, these come in hues of red, orange, yellow, or white, and can be grown for cut flowers.
♠ 30–100cm (1–3ft)
⬧ 30cm (12in)

9 Zinnias These exotic-looking annuals provide colour in late summer. They are good cut flowers.
♠ 30–100cm (1–3ft)
⬧ 30cm (12in)

10 Cosmos Easy to grow from seed, these are excellent in borders, and flower into autumn.
♠ 60cm (2ft) ⬧ 30cm (1ft)

Rosa 'Fragrant Cloud'

Roses

A must for any garden, plant species, *Rosa,* encompasses a large and varied group of shrubs. There are thousands of roses to choose, ranging from compact varieties for containers, useful ground-cover forms, shrubby types for borders, to climbers and ramblers for walls and fences. Many are richly fragrant, others flower continually until the first hard frosts, and some also have decorative hips for autumn interest. Roses are easy to care for. Simply mulch plants in spring, deadhead during summer, and prune them in autumn or winter.

AT A GLANCE
- ❦ **Plant type** Hardy shrub/climber
- ☘ **Height** 30cm–12m (1–40ft)
- 🍃 **Spread** 60cm–4m (2–12ft)
- ☼ **Aspect** Full sun
- ◉ **Soil type** Fertile and moist

Which to choose

Roses are commonly referred to as being either "hybrid tea" or "floribunda" varieties, which refers to their flowers and how they are produced.

Hybrid tea roses, like 'Poetry in Motion' (*above*) and 'Fragrant Cloud' (*left*), bear one large flower at the end of each stem. They are good for cutting.

Floribunda roses, also known as "cluster roses", produce a group of flowers at the end of each stem. 'Princess of Wales' (*above*) is one example.

Choosing roses

Roses all enjoy the same conditions, so deciding which to grow is a matter of taste. As a general rule, modern varieties flower more freely than old-fashioned types, and have good disease resistance. However, older varieties often have the finest scents. Rambling roses can grow very large, and bloom in a beautiful, but single, flush. Climbing varieties are less rampant but can flower throughout summer. Deadhead roses for the best show.

R. 'Complicata'
(shrub)

R. 'Sandringham
Centenary'
(shrub)

Rosa 'Blush
Damask'
(shrub)

Containers

Roses grow well in containers as long as they are watered and fed regularly. Choose a pot at least 25cm (10in) or more deep, and ensure it has ample drainage holes. Miniature or patio varieties, such as 'Hand in Hand' (*left*) are the best choices. Plant into soil-based compost and position the container in a sunny site.

Ground cover

Some roses have a spreading habit, and either hug the soil or form a low mound, making them ideal to grow as ground cover. They are particularly useful for covering large or awkward areas, such as slopes. Varieties include any from the Flower Carpet series, like 'White' (*left*), or the County series, such as 'Worcestershire'.

R. 'Dorothy
Perkins'
(rambler)

R. centifolia
(shrub)

R. 'Westerland'
(shrub)

R. 'Ferdinand
Pichard'
(shrub)

Autumn hips

If left in place, and not
deadheaded after blooming
in summer, the flowers of a
number of shrub roses develop
into attractive hips in autumn,
giving two seasons of interest.
Good choices for colourful
fruits are R. gallica, R. moysii
(left), and R. rugosa, which
have pink, red, or white
flowers, and orange-red hips.

Climbers

Climbing and rambling roses
are ideal for growing up
vertical surfaces and over
garden buildings. Rambling
roses are vigorous, and best
grown over larger structures,
and even through trees.
Climbing roses are ideal for
fences, arches, and arbours,
where their flowers can be
enjoyed at eye level.

Runner bean 'Scarlet Emperor'

Garden beans

French and runner beans crop abundantly during summer – just 12 plants will be plenty for a small family. Being climbing plants, they are ideal to grow where space is limited, and can be even be planted in large containers. Prepare the soil by digging in garden compost and provide a suitable support, such as a wigwam of tall canes. Seed can be sown into single pots in mid-spring under cover for an early crop, or directly into the ground in early summer. Tie the seedlings to their canes at first to train them up, and keep them well watered throughout summer. When the plants have reached the top of their supports, pinch out the tips to encourage growth further down. Pick the pods while young and tender, and do so regularly to encourage more to grow.

AT A GLANCE
- ❀ **Plant type** Annual
- ☀ **Aspect** Full sun
- ◎ **Soil type** Fertile and moist
- ↓ **Sow seed** Mid-spring – early summer
- ◎ **Harvest** Midsummer – early autumn

Which to choose

French and runner beans are grown in the same way. Unless you have a preference between the two, grow both types on the same support.

Runner beans produce long, flattened pods that are harvested while young and tender, before the beans inside are fully developed.

French beans produce slim, pencil-like pods. Harvest them as soon as they are big enough to use. Dwarf varieties can be grown in pots.

Viburnum opulus 'Roseum'

Viburnums

The summer-flowering forms of these deciduous shrubs are among the first to bloom after spring, and give an elegant display of white flowers, sometimes flushed with pink. These appear as rounded globes or flat, frilly lacecaps, and last for many weeks. Viburnums are large shrubs but many, such as *V. opulus*, also develop attractive berries and colourful foliage in autumn, so certainly earn their place in the garden. Easy to grow on most soils, established shrubs need little care. Mulch plants during spring and prune them after flowering has finished to remove any wayward stems, and dead, weak, or diseased growth.

AT A GLANCE

- ❦ **Plant type** Hardy shrub
- ⚘ **Height** 1–5m (3–15ft)
- ◣ **Spread** 1–5m (3–15ft)
- ☀ **Aspect** Full sun or partial shade
- ◉ **Soil type** Fertile, moist, well drained

Which to choose

Viburnum opulus gives interest in summer and autumn, and is a good choice for most gardens. 'Roseum' (*left*) has pretty pompon-like blooms.

'**Compactum**' (*above*) is a dense, mound-forming variety, suitable for smaller gardens. It reaches just 1.5m (5ft) in height and spread.

'**Xanthocarpum**' (*above*) bears white lacecap blooms followed by bright berries that ripen to yellow from summer into autumn.

Courgette 'Defender'

Courgettes

One of the most abundant crops to grow, you
can look forward to harvesting 3 or 4 plump
courgettes per plant each week in summer.
They are easy plants to grow but require a lot
of space, so don't grow more than you really
need – they can also be grown in pots if kept
very well watered. Seeds are sown under cover
in spring or outside in early summer, 2.5cm
(1in) deep. Dig in plenty of organic matter
before planting and keep plants well watered.
Pick courgettes a few days after they appear,
while they are still small and tender. They
crop rapidly, so check plants almost daily.

AT A GLANCE
❧ **Plant type** Annual
☀ **Aspect** Full sun
◉ **Soil type** Fertile and moist
∨ **Sow seed** Mid-spring – early summer
◎ **Harvest** Midsummer – late summer

Growing advice

If kept well watered throughout summer, courgettes can provide three crops in one. Some varieties have a trailing habit – train them along the ground to keep them tidy.

Courgette flowers are delicious stuffed and fried. Harvest the male, non-fruiting blooms, which are those without fruitlets behind their petals. Pick them in bud.

Yellow courgettes are easier to spot among the leaves, meaning you are less likely to miss any while young and tender. They taste the same as green varieties.

Unpicked courgettes grow into large, thick-skinned marrows. Although these are a tasty crop, they are used differently from courgettes. You can also expect fewer fruits per plant. To grow marrows, thin to 2–3 per plant and harvest in summer.

Raspberry 'Malling Jewel'
(summer-fruiting)

Raspberries

These sweet and juicy fruits are simple to
grow, and you don't require many plants for
a good crop. Raspberries are divided into two
types, summer- and autumn-fruiting. Plant
varieties of each and enjoy a harvest from
midsummer to the first frosts. The berries are
loved by birds, so net plants before they start
to ripen. For the best crop, water them well
and mulch in spring with compost. The plants
also require support and pruning (*see below*).

Growing advice

Raspberry canes require support as they grow, so are planted in
rows next to two or three horizontal wires stretched between posts
(*see below*). Regularly tie in the canes to the wires using soft string.

To prune summer-fruiting raspberries, cut all fruited canes to
the base and tie the unfruited canes to their support. Prune
autumn-fruiting varieties completely to the base in late winter.

AT A GLANCE
🌱 **Plant type** Hardy shrub
🌿 **Height** 1.5–2.5m (5–8ft)
🍃 **Spread** 30–60cm (1–2ft)
☼ **Aspect** Full sun or partial shade
⊚ **Soil type** Fertile and moist
◎ **Harvest** Midsummer – mid-autumn

Flowering plants for Garden ponds

Ponds make ideal wildlife habitats, but can also be highly decorative, harbouring colourful plants throughout summer. Aquatic plants also help to keep the water clear and healthy by shading the surface and releasing oxygen.

1 *Nymphaea odorata* With their showy flowers in many shades, waterlilies are planted in the pond. Position 15–100cm (6–39in) deep. ◣ 15cm–4m (6in–12ft)

2 *Ranunculus flammula* This free-flowering perennial is ideal for planting at the pond margin. ♠ 70cm (28in) ◣ 75cm (30in)

3 *Mimulus cardinalis* The scarlet monkey flower is a colourful addition to the pond margin. ♠ 60cm (2ft) ◣ 60cm (2ft)

4 *Eriophorum angustifolium* Known as cotton grass, it bears fluffy white flowers during summer. It is suitable for pond edges. ♠ 30cm (1ft) ◣ 1m (3ft)

5 *Calla palustris* Best at the water's edge, it has large glossy leaves and arum lily-like flowers. ♠ 25cm (10in) ◣ 60cm (24in)

6 *Pontederia cordata* Known as pickerel weed, this marginal plant has spires of blue flowers. It is especially attractive to dragonflies. ♠ 90cm (36in) ◣ 75cm (30in)

7 *Typha minima* This miniature bullrush is ideal for the margin of smaller ponds. It has a tendency to spread, so plant it in a basket. ♠ 75cm (30in) ◣ 30cm (12in)

8 *Iris laevigata* This beautiful iris flowers in midsummer, and forms a clump at the pond's edge. ♠ 2m (6ft) ◣ 2m (6ft)

9 *Orontium aquaticum* Planted in the water, it has floating leaves and spikes of yellow flowers. ♠ 45cm (18in) ◣ 75cm (30in)

10 *Zantedeschia aethiopica* The arum lily has large glossy leaves and beautiful white flowers. Plant it at the pond's edge. ♠ 60cm (2ft) ◣ 30cm (1ft)

Lilium 'Venezuela'
(oriental)

Lilies

These summer-flowering bulbs provide
elegantly sculpted flowers, many of which are
intoxicatingly fragrant, for several weeks in
summer. Suitable for borders and containers,
Lilium, as they are properly named, flower in
a huge array of colours, from pure white to
blackish red. There is also a surprisingly wide
variation in the size, markings, and shape of
the flowers. Plant bulbs in spring, keep them
well watered once growth starts, and feed
them fortnightly with tomato fertilizer. Taller
varieties, especially Turk's-cap types, require
support. Remove spent flowers and allow the
foliage to die back naturally in autumn.

AT A GLANCE
❀ **Plant type** Hardy bulb
❀ **Height** 60cm–1.5m (2–5ft)
❀ **Spread** 15–100cm (6–39in)
❀ **Aspect** Full sun or dappled shade
❀ **Soil type** Fertile and well drained

Planting partners

Lilies need to continue growing after flowering, so plant them near other plants that can help to disguise them, and also provide further colour.

Verbena bonariensis is a tall, branching perennial that flowers from midsummer to autumn. Grow it with taller lily varieties.

Montbretia, *Crocosmia* x *crocosmiiflora*, flowers in late summer and provides border interest after most shorter lilies have faded.

Choosing lilies

Lilies are mostly grown in a similar way, and there are four main flower types to choose from. Asiatic lilies have open, upwards or outwards-facing blooms, which are unscented. Turk's-cap types are sometimes scented, and bear abundant smaller blooms on a branched stem. Oriental lilies produce very large and fragrant flowers with broad petals, while the trumpet lilies are also highly scented, but have deep-throated blooms.

Lilium 'Star Gazer' (oriental)

L. regale (trumpet)

In the garden

Lilies are fully hardy and can be left in the ground over winter as long as it isn't prone to waterlogging. If undisturbed, many lilies form clumps over time, which should be divided every three years to maintain their vigour (*see p.261*). Feed lily clumps by mulching them in spring.

L. 'Red Night'
(asiatic)

L. 'Citronella'
(Turk's cap)

Cauliflower 'Tarifa'

Summer cauliflowers

This brassica is a staple of the Sunday roast, and is commonly harvested from midsummer to autumn, although there are year-round varieties. It is easy to grow, but as these are large, slow-maturing plants, this crop is best reserved for bigger plots with very rich soil. Seed can be sown in a prepared seedbed or under cover in modules, then transplanted to their final positions. Alternatively, buy young plants from a garden centre. As the "curds" (the flowerheads) form, cover them with some of the plant's own leaves to retain their pale colour (*see p.195*). Keep plants well watered, and harvest once the heads reach a good size.

Which to choose

In addition to the conventional white-headed cauliflowers, there are also attractive coloured forms. These are grown in the same way and can be used to add interest to cooked dishes.

Purple cauliflowers are rich in the same antioxidant that is found in red cabbage, and some retain their colour once cooked. Varieties to try include 'Purple Graffiti' (*above*).

Romanesco cauliflower has unusual lime-green heads that develop into jagged peaks. It has a crisper texture than traditional varieties, and matures from late summer.

AT A GLANCE
- ❧ **Plant type** Hardy annual
- ☀ **Aspect** Full sun
- ⊛ **Soil type** Fertile and moist
- ↧ **Sow seed** Early spring – mid-spring
- ◎ **Harvest** Midsummer – mid-autumn

Sweet pea 'Spencer Mixed'

Sweet peas

These beautifully scented climbing annuals fill the air with fragrance, and are ideal adding summer colour to fences or supports. They are also an excellent source of cut flowers – the more they are cut, the more they produce new blooms. Seeds can be sown under cover in autumn in milder areas to flower earlier; otherwise wait until spring. Pinch out young plants to encourage plenty of flowering stems, and water them frequently during dry spells. Deadhead any spent flowers regularly.

Which to choose

In addition to the climbing varieties, there are also dwarf forms that can be grown in containers.

The perennial sweet pea, *Lathyrus latifolius*, is as free-flowering as the annual forms and just as attractive. However, the blooms are smaller and unscented.

AT A GLANCE
- ❦ **Plant type** Hardy annual
- ☘ **Height** 30cm–2.5m (1–8ft)
- ☙ **Spread** 30–45cm (12–18in)
- ☀ **Aspect** Full sun
- ◉ **Soil type** Moist and well drained
- ⋎ **Sow seed** Autumn – early spring

Globe artichoke
'Purple Globe'

Globe artichokes

Decorative as well as edible, these gourmet vegetables need plenty of space but are attractive enough to grow in flower beds. Best bought as young plants in spring, one should produce around ten edible heads in its second year. Globe artichokes are perennials, so will come back year after year. Keep plants well watered and weed-free, and mulch with garden compost each spring. To maintain their vigour, divide plants every three years (*see p.261*).

Growing advice

Harvest the flowers once the scaly buds are fully formed but before they start to open. They become inedible if left too long.

After harvesting, leave the plants to grow until autumn before cutting back the stems. Although hardy, the plants benefit from a thick mulch of compost over their crown.

AT A GLANCE
- ☙ **Plant type** Hardy perennial
- ⚘ **Height** 1.5–2m (5–6ft)
- ☙ **Spread** 1–1.2m (3–4ft)
- ☀ **Aspect** Full sun
- ☷ **Soil type** Fertile and moist
- ◎ **Harvest** Early summer

Salvia x *superba* 'East Friesland'

Perennial salvias

Flowering throughout summer in vivid shades of white, pink, blue, and red, these perennials are an excellent addition to a sunny border. All have an upright habit, producing slender stems of tubular blooms that are a magnet for bees and butterflies. Some species are fully hardy but most are slightly tender, so should be protected during winter. In milder areas, mulch around plants with garden compost or straw to protect the roots. In colder regions, lift and move them under cover until spring.

AT A GLANCE
🌿 **Plant type** Hardy/half hardy perennial
🌱 **Height** 30cm–1.2m (1–4ft)
🍃 **Spread** 30–100cm (1–3ft)
☀ **Aspect** Full sun
◉ **Soil type** Well drained

Which to choose

S. x **superba** is a hardy perennial with purple flowers from midsummer. Varieties include 'East Friesland' (*left*). It grows to 90 x 60cm (3 x 2ft).

S. x **jamensis** is a large shrubby plant that flowers in a wide range of colours. It requires protection during winter. Varieties include 'Hot Lips' (*above*).

S. microphylla flowers in late summer bearing vivid blooms like those of 'Robin's Pride' (*above*). It has a bushy habit and needs winter protection.

S. greggii is a low-growing, shrubby perennial. There are many colourful varieties, including 'Navajo Cream' (*above*). Protect during winter.

Garlic 'Purple Wight'

Growing advice

To grow garlic, only buy certified bulbs at the garden centre or by mail order. Culinary bulbs sold in supermarkets are unsuited to our climate.

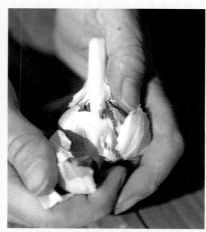

Garlic bulbs are supplied whole and should be divided into individual cloves for planting. Avoid damaging the outer skins of the cloves.

Plant into small pots if conditions outside are unfavourable. Allow them to root, then plant them out when the weather allows.

Garlic

The essential ingredient in many dishes, garlic is straightforward and rewarding to grow, with each clove developing into a whole bulb. As it is planted in autumn and grows through the winter, it is easy to find space for it in empty plots, flower beds, or even containers. Plant the cloves directly where they are to grow, 10cm (4in) apart, with their tips just below the soil surface. Cover with cloches or fleece in frosty weather, and keep plants well watered during dry weather as the bulbs form. Harvest in midsummer, once the leaves have turned yellow, carefully digging up the bulbs with a fork. The bulbs can then be dried and plaited, ready to store (*see pp.146–147* and *p.194*).

AT A GLANCE
- ☙ **Plant type** Hardy annual
- ☀ **Aspect** Full sun
- ◉ **Soil type** Well drained
- ⋎ **Plant cloves** Mid-autumn – winter
- ◎ **Harvest** Early summer – late summer

Climbers for
Vertical colour

Flowering climbers provide drama, colour, and scent to the garden, and are invaluable for covering ugly fences or walls. Some, such as passion flower, are self-clinging and attach themselves to surfaces, while many others, including honeysuckle, need regular training and tying in to keep them tidy.

1 *Schizophragma integrifolium* The Chinese hydrangea vine has showy white flowers, and is ideal for a shady wall or fence, or an old tree.
🌱 10m (30ft) ◣ 4m (12ft)

2 *Jasminum officinale* Jasmine has wonderfully scented white flowers. It needs a warm position.
🌱 3m (10ft) ◣ 2.5m (8ft)

3 *Thunbergia alata* Annual black-eyed Susan will quickly cover a trellis or obelisk in colour.
🌱 2.5m (8ft) ◣ 1m (3ft)

4 *Trachelospermum jasminoides* An evergreen with richly scented flowers, it needs warmth and shelter.
🌱 8m (25ft) ◣ 8m (25ft)

5 *Eccremocarpus scaber* Exotic-looking Chilean glory is tender but fast-growing. It can be grown from seed and treated as an annual.
🌱 3m (10ft) ◣ 1m (3ft)

6 *Passiflora caerulea* The hardy passion flower has eye-catching blooms in summer followed by decorative orange fruits in autumn.
🌱 5m (15ft) ◣ 4m (12ft)

7 *Wisteria floribunda* Bearing chains of fragrant flowers, this vigorous shrub needs something sturdy to climb, and ample space.
🌱 9m (28ft) ◣ 1.5m (5ft)

8 *Ipomoea purpurea* Annual morning glory is grown from seed, and flowers abundantly in sun.
🌱 2.5m (8ft) ◣ 2m (6ft)

9 *Tropaeolum majus* Grown from seed, annual nasturtiums trail or climb, and flower very freely.
🌱 1.8m (6ft) ◣ 1.8m (6ft)

10 *Lonicera periclymenum* Fragrant honeysuckle is a great choice for a wall or fence in a cottage or wildlife garden.
🌱 7m (22ft) ◣ 1.5m (5ft)

Shallot 'Golden Gourmet'

Onions and shallots

Onions and shallots are kitchen essentials and very easy to grow. They're usually raised from "sets" – small bulbs – planted in early spring (*see p.73*). Each onion set grows into a larger bulb, while a shallot set produces 6–8 shallots. Plant onions 10cm (4in) apart, shallots 25cm (10in) apart, with their tips set just above the soil surface. Weed regularly and water during dry spells. Harvest when the leafy tops have turned yellow and start to flop over (*see p.194*).

Which to choose

Onions are larger than shallots and grow as individual bulbs (*see below*). They have a stronger flavour, and have either red or white flesh.

Shallots develop as small clusters of bulbs (*see right*) that are harvested together, then separated. The bulbs can be round or torpedo-shaped, and some varieties have pink-tinged flesh.

AT A GLANCE
- ❦ **Plant type** Hardy biennial
- ☼ **Aspect** Full sun
- ☺ **Soil type** Well drained
- ⩔ **Plant sets** Early spring – late spring
- ◎ **Harvest** Midsummer – mid-autumn

Make: A garlic plait

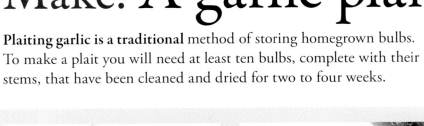

Plaiting garlic is a traditional method of storing homegrown bulbs. To make a plait you will need at least ten bulbs, complete with their stems, that have been cleaned and dried for two to four weeks.

1 Trim the roots and brush the bulbs clean. On a flat surface, lay the first stem in the centre with two others then crossing it from the left then right (*see above*).

3 When all bulbs are added, divide the stems on the left, right, and centre of the plait into three strands. Try to avoid disturbing the cluster of bulbs at this stage.

4 Plait the stems, passing the strands right-over-centre, then left-over-centre until the whole stem is plaited. Apply an even tension for a neat finish, and tie the end using string.

2 Lay three more bulbs over the first trio, this time crossing the central stem from the right then left. Continue adding stems, alternating the direction they cross over.

HELPFUL TIP
The best garlic for plaiting are "softneck" varieties. These can be stored for longer than "hardneck" types, and have pliable stems that are more easily plaited.

5 Hang the plait in a cool, airy place, like a shed, for 2–3 weeks to dry the bulb skins and stems. It can then be brought indoors to use as required.

Red currant
'Jonkheer van Tets'

Red, white, and black currants

Whichever colour you prefer, currants crop prolifically once established, bearing sweet, sharp-tasting berries from midsummer. Just one or two plants can provide all the fruit you need, which can be eaten fresh or used in cooking. Keep plants well watered and mulch with garden compost in spring. To deter birds, net plants before the fruit starts to ripen, or it will soon vanish. To encourage fruiting, prune plants in summer and winter (*see p.191*).

AT A GLANCE
❧ **Plant type** Hardy shrub
🌱 **Height** 1.5–2m (5–6ft)
🌿 **Spread** 1.5–2m (5–6ft)
☀ **Aspect** Full sun or partial shade
☺ **Soil type** Fertile and free draining
◎ **Harvest** Midsummer – late summer

White currant
'Versailles Blanche'

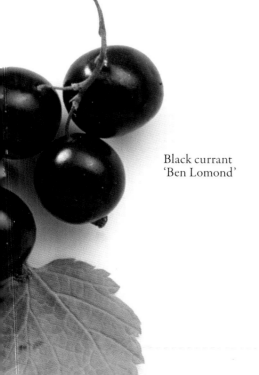

Black currant
'Ben Lomond'

Growing advice

Although they are closely related, black currants are planted and cared for slightly differently from red- or white currants.

To plant black currants, plant the crown below soil level. Red- and white currants are planted proud of the soil surface.

Black currant bushes become laden with berries, which can damage younger fruiting stems. Insert canes for support.

Modern black currants, such as those with "Ben" is their name, ripen as whole "sprigs" (*above*), which makes picking them easy. Older varieties are harvested as individual berries.

Cabbage 'Greyhound'

Summer Cabbages

This is a tasty and versatile vegetable that can be harvested throughout summer and autumn. It is slow-growing, however, and requires a lot of space, so is best reserved for larger gardens. Sow seed into a seedbed or in trays under cover, before transplanting the young plants to their final positions, 30–45cm (12–18in) apart, in early summer. Keep the plants well-watered and, once they reach a usable size, harvest the heads by cutting through the stem.

Growing advice

Cover plants with insect-proof mesh after planting to prevent attack from birds and the caterpillars of cabbage white butterflies.

If left in the ground after harvesting, cabbage stumps may resprout. Encourage this by cutting a cross in the cut end.

AT A GLANCE

❋ **Plant type** Hardy biennial

☼ **Aspect** Partial shade

◉ **Soil type** Fertile and moist

↓ **Sow seed** Early spring – late spring

◎ **Harvest** Late summer – late autumn

Plants to attract
Bees and butterflies

Bees and butterflies play a vital role in the garden, pollinating flowers and enabling crops to set their fruit. They are also highly attractive, bringing natural sound, colour, and life. To encourage them into your garden, grow plants rich in nectar with simple, colourful blooms that are highly visible and give easy access for insects.

1 *Limnanthes douglasii* Annual poached-egg plant grows very quickly from seed and flowers freely.
🌱 15cm (6in) ◣ 15cm (6in)

2 *Echinacea purpurea* This attractive perennial has pink or yellow flowers from midsummer.
🌱 1m (3ft) ◣ 60cm (2ft)

3 *Centaurea montana* Perennial knapweed bears spidery blue flowers from early- to midsummer.
🌱 45cm (18in) ◣ 60cm (24in)

4 *Buddleja davidii* Known as butterfly bush, this vigorous shrub is by far the best plant you can grow to attract butterflies.
🌱 4m (12ft) ◣ 4m (12ft)

5 *Monarda didyma* Known as bee balm, this perennial has white, red, or pink summer flowers. There are many varieties to choose.
🌱 90cm (3ft) ◣ 45cm (18in)

6 *Campanula persicifolia* This evergreen perennial bears dainty bell-shaped blooms in early summer.
🌱 90cm (3ft) ◣ 30cm (1ft)

7 *Calendula officinalis* Annual pot marigolds are good for cutting. The flowers are edible.
🌱 45cm (18in) ◣ 30cm (12in)

8 *Verbena bonariensis* This tall, graceful perennial flowers all summer on elegant wiry stems.
🌱 1m (3ft) ◣ 30cm (1ft)

9 *Echinops ritro* Globe thistle is a large upright perennial, and a good source of flowers for cutting.
🌱 90cm (3ft) ◣ 60cm (2ft)

10 *Cephalaria gigantea* Ideal for the back of a border, this imposing perennial has branching stems of yellow flowers. Bees love it.
🌱 1.8m (6ft) ◣ 1m (3ft)

Cucumber 'Burpless Tasty Green'

Cucumbers

A vital ingredient for summer salads, these succulent fruits are divided into smooth-skinned greenhouse varieties, and outdoor "ridge" types, which have textured skins. Greenhouse varieties climb, and are trained up canes or strings. Once they reach the top, pinch out their tips. When the fruits begin to develop, pinch out the end of each sideshoot, leaving two leaves after each fruit. Outdoor types are planted directly in the soil, and either sprawl across the ground or can be trained up supports to save space. To encourage fruiting, pinch out the main stem after seven leaves have formed. Water cucumbers very frequently and feed them weekly with tomato fertilizer.

AT A GLANCE
- ❦ **Plant type** Annual
- ☀ **Aspect** Full sun
- ◎ **Soil type** Fertile and moist
- ⋎ **Sow seed** Mid-spring – early summer
- ◎ **Harvest** Midsummer – mid autumn

Growing advice

Although greenhouse and outdoor cucumbers have different growth habits and differing fruits, some tasks are common to growing both types.

Male flowers are not required and should be removed as they appear. These are the blooms that don't have a fruitlet behind their petals.

Harvest cucumbers once they reach a usable size and while they are still tender. Cut the tough fruit stalks using scissors or secateurs.

Fuchsia 'Heidi Ann'

Fuschias

These colourful shrubs have beautiful, long-lasting flowers and are easy to grow, making them very popular. There is a huge range of varieties, from tender bedding plants for pots and hanging baskets, to hardy shrubs to grow in the border – some can even be used as a hedge. Best shaded from the hottest part of the day, water them generously, and shelter them from cold winds. Tender varieties should be brought under cover in autumn. If you haven't space for mature plants indoors, take semi-ripe cuttings in summer (*see pp.194–195*) to bring inside instead. In colder areas, hardy fuchsias benefit from being mulched with compost during autumn to help protect their roots.

AT A GLANCE
- ❦ **Plant type** Hardy/half hardy shrub
- ⚘ **Height** 15cm–2m (6in–6ft)
- ❧ **Spread** 30cm–1.5m (1–5ft)
- ☀ **Aspect** Full sun or dappled shade
- ⊚ **Soil type** Fertile, moist, well drained

Which to choose

Hardy fuchsias make excellent border shrubs and flower for weeks, although their blooms are small and simple compared to the tender hybrids. These require winter protection under cover, however.

Hardy fuchsias include individually named hybrids, such as 'Heidi Ann' (*left*), and the many varieties of *F. magellanica* (*above*).

Tender fuchsias flower in a wider range of colours and styles than hardy types. 'Orange King' (*above*) is a trailing form for baskets.

Tomato 'Gardener's Delight'

Tomatoes

From cherry-sized to large beefsteaks, this is one of the most popular crops to grow. There are hundreds to choose, from the latest hybrids to fascinating "heirloom" tomatoes. All require sunlight and warmth to crop well, and are ideal for greenhouses and growing frames, although some can also be grown outside in bright, sheltered spots. Plant them directly into the soil or into growing bags or pots. Tomatoes can be grown from seed in spring, which gives the best range of varieties, or bought as young plants. Keep them well watered and feed them with high-potash tomato fertilizer every week once the first flowers appear. Plants can crop freely, so check them daily for the best harvest.

AT A GLANCE
- ❧ **Plant type** Annual
- ☀ **Aspect** Full sun
- ◉ **Soil type** Fertile and moist
- ⋎ **Sow seed** Early spring – mid-spring
- ◎ **Harvest** Midsummer – mid-autumn

'Golden Pearl'
(cherry)

'Whipper Snapper'
(cherry)

Choosing tomatoes

Tomatoes are divided into two groups, cordon and bush varieties. Cordon varieties
are trained as a single stem *(see right)* and usually grown under cover. Bush varieties
have multiple stems and are commonly grown outside. The fruits range greatly in
colour, size, flavour, and fleshiness. Choose the right type for your garden,
and a variety that suits your taste.

'Beefeater'
(beefsteak)

'Ananas Noire'
(heirloom)

'Gardener's Delight'
(large cherry)

Growing advice

Supporting

Cordon tomatoes are grown as
a single stem supported by a cane
or vertical string. Provide the
support when the tomato is first
planted and tie the stem to it as
it grows. If using a string support,
carefully wind the stem around it.
Bush tomatoes have many stems
that will all need support. Insert
as many canes as are necessary
and tie the stems to them.

Sideshoots

Tomatoes naturally produce
sideshoots at the joints between
their main stems and leaf stalks.
On bush types, these are allowed
to develop and require supporting
(*see above*). When growing cordon
varieties, pinch out any sideshoots
that form while they are still small.
Also remove their main growing
tip once the plant reaches the top
of its support (*see p.195*).

Harvesting

Tomatoes quickly spoil if left
on the plant too long, so harvest
them regularly, and don't rely on
their shade to indicate ripeness.
Although most tomatoes ripen
red, others turn yellow, green, or
black. A tomato is ready to pick as
soon as you can pull it easily from
the truss at the "knuckle". This is
the swollen bump on the stem
where the fruit is attached.

Plum 'Victoria'
(dual purpose)

Plums

A delightful feature in the garden, a plum tree provides pretty blossom in spring and an abundant summer harvest. Varieties are either culinary or dessert types, but a few are dual-purpose, suitable for cooking and eating fresh. Many are also self-fertile and available on dwarfing rootstocks so, even if you only have space available for one tree, you will be able to enjoy a crop of plums. For the best harvest, position the tree in a sheltered spot to protect the blossom from frost. Mulch in spring with compost, and in summer, thin the young fruit (*see p.193*), and prune the tree (*see p.197*). Plums are best picked when ripe and soft.

AT A GLANCE
- ❧ **Plant type** Hardy deciduous tree
- ♠ **Height** 2–3m (6–10ft)
- 🍃 **Spread** 2–3m (6–10ft)
- ☀ **Aspect** Full sun
- ◉ **Soil type** Fertile, moist, well drained
- ◎ **Harvest** Midsummer – mid-autumn

Which to choose

In addition to being suitable for cooking or eating fresh, plums are also divided into gages, damsons, and bullaces, each of which have their own qualities.

Damsons are smaller than plums. With a sharper taste, they are best eaten cooked. Varieties include 'Merryweather' (*above*). All have a dark skin.

Gages have a rich, sweet flavour, and can be eaten fresh or cooked. They are green or yellow in colour. Varieties include 'Old Green Gage' (*above*).

Bullaces are smaller than damsons, with a yellow or purple skin. They can be eaten fresh when very ripe. Varieties include 'Langley Bullace' (*above*).

Aubergine 'Black Enorma'

Aubergines

A taste of the Mediterranean, these plump and glossy fruits need plenty of heat and sunlight to do well, so are best grown in a greenhouse or on a sunny, sheltered patio. Large, purple-fruited varieties are the most familiar, although aubergines come in various colours, shapes, and sizes. Grow them from seed sown under cover in spring or buy young plants. Plant them into large containers or growing bags, and provide support. Pinch out their tips when 30cm (12in) tall to encourage branching. Water regularly and feed fortnightly after the first flowers appear. The fruits are picked when shiny and firm, and before they turn cloudy.

AT A GLANCE
- ❧ **Plant type** Annual
- ☀ **Aspect** Full sun
- ⊕ **Soil type** Compost or growing bag
- ↓ **Sow seed** Early spring – mid-spring
- ◎ **Harvest** Late summer – mid-autumn

Which to choose

There are various aubergine varieties to try that can all be grown in the same way. Consider growing more than one variety and enjoy a mix of aubergine types.

White aubergines understandably gave rise to the common name, eggplant. Plants and seeds are not widely sold but varieties available include 'Snowy'.

Striped varieties taste the same as white or purple aubergines, but add interest to cooked dishes. Varieties include 'Listade de Gandia' (*above*).

Penstemon 'Countess of Dalkeith'

Penstemons

These elegant, upright perennials bloom from summer to autumn, bearing spikes of tubular flowers in a wide variety of cool or vibrant shades, from electric blue to deep scarlet. The boldest plants are the taller varieties, which are ideal for borders and containers, while compact forms give a good display on rockeries. For a prolonged show, deadhead regularly, stake taller plants, and water during dry spells. Not all penstemons are hardy, but new plants can easily be grown from cuttings (*see pp.194–195*). If kept under cover during winter, the cuttings will flower the following summer. In colder areas, mulch around plants growing outside to protect their roots.

Which to choose

The best varieties for stunning border displays are those that grow to at least 60cm (2ft) tall. These include 'Countess of Dalkeith' (*right*).

'White Bedder' gives a cool display from midsummer to mid-autumn. Plant it near darker varieties for maximum impact.

'Pensham Czar' bears spikes of purple-blue flowers with contrasting white throats. It is a good choice for containers if fed regularly.

'Chester Scarlet' has slender, crimson blooms and flowers freely, creating a spectacular show. It is a tall choice, reaching 1m (3ft) in height.

AT A GLANCE
- ❧ **Plant type** Hardy/half hardy perennial
- ☖ **Height** 45cm–1.8m (18in–6ft)
- ☖ **Spread** 30–50cm (12–20in)
- ☀ **Aspect** Full sun or partial shade
- ☺ **Soil type** Fertile and well drained

Lavandula angustifolia

Lavender

Richly scented, adored by bees, and free-flowering, this versatile evergreen shrub is equally at home in modern and traditional garden styles. It is native to the Mediterranean, and needs plenty of sunshine and well drained soil to grow well, but can be short-lived. Use it as an informal hedge or to line a path, or plant it *en masse* to create a stunning display of colour and to concentrate the fragrance. Compact forms are also ideal for containers, used to bring scent nearer to the house. Lavender, or *Lavandula*, tolerates drought and requires little care after planting. Simply give it a light prune after flowering to maintain it (*see p.201*).

AT A GLANCE
- ❦ **Plant type** Evergreen shrub
- ❦ **Height** 60–100cm (2–3ft)
- ❦ **Spread** 60cm–1.5m (2–5ft)
- ☀ **Aspect** Full sun
- ◉ **Soil type** Well drained

Which to choose

English lavender, *L. angustifolia*, is the most
widely grown, but there are other species. These
are equally attractive but need winter protection.

French lavender, *L. stoechas*, is a knee-high
shrub with flag-like "bracts" on top of its
flowers. Short-lived, treat it as bedding.

Mound-forming *L. dentata* bears pale
purple flowers from mid- to late summer.
Its height and spread is 1 x 1.5m (3 x 5ft).

Ferny leaved *L. pinnata* produces trident-like
spikes of purple-blue flowers on long stems.
It grows to 1m (3ft) in height and spread.

Perennial plants for
Cut flowers

Picking homegrown flowers for the house is a gardener's perk, and many perennials look as good in the vase as they do in the garden. Cutting flowers encourages most perennials to produce more blooms, although don't pick so many that you spoil the display outside. To help them last, cut the flowers in the morning.

1 *Rudbeckia laciniata* This plant has long-lasting yellow flowers. 'Goldquelle' (*left*) has double blooms.
↕ 1m (3ft) ↔ 60cm (2ft)

2 *Helenium autumnale* The flowers of this late-summer perennial last for a week in water.
↕ 1m (3ft) ↔ 60cm (2ft)

3 *Leucanthemum* x *superbum* These simple white daisies look stunning planted in drifts in the garden, or cut in a vase indoors.
↕ 90cm (36in) ↔ 50cm (20in)

4 *Dianthus caryophyllus* Unlike carnations bought at a florist's, garden blooms are richly scented.
↕ 50cm (20in) ↔ 20cm (8in)

5 *Alstroemeria aurea* Peruvian lilies bring a touch of the exotic to a garden border and can last up to three weeks as cut flowers.
↕ 1m (3ft) ↔ 45cm (18in)

6 *Phlox paniculata* Loved by bees, this tall favourite of the cottage garden and herbaceous bed fills a room with delicious scent.
↕ 1m (3ft) ↔ 60cm (2ft)

7 *Liatris spicata* Flowering in late summer, it bears tall spikes of pink, mauve, or white blooms.
↕ 1.5m (5ft) ↔ 45cm (18in)

8 *Paeonia lactiflora* Peonies can be short-lived in a vase but it's a great way to enjoy their exquisite pink, white, or red blooms.
↕ 50cm (20in) ↔ 70cm (28in)

9 *Crocosmia* x *crocosmiiflora* These fiery beauties look good planted in swathes in the garden, and can last two weeks in a vase.
↕ 60cm (24in) ↔ 15cm (6in)

10 *Astrantia major* Bees love the unusual-looking flowers of this cottage-garden plant. They last well in water after cutting.
↕ 70cm (28in) ↔ 45cm (18in)

Chilli 'Hot Mexican'

Chillies

Attractive and highly productive,
chillies are easy to grow and are ideal
for pots. The plants need warmth and
sunlight to produce the largest crops,
so are best grown in a greenhouse
or on a sunny windowsill or patio.
The fruits range greatly in size, shape,
colour, and spiciness, and there are
hundreds of varieties to choose. Sow
seeds under cover in early spring or
buy young plants, and grow them
in containers or growing bags with
support. Pinch out young plants
when 30cm (12in) tall to encourage
bushiness, water regularly, and feed
with tomato fertilizer every fortnight
after the first flowers appear. Pick the
first few fruits while still green to
encourage more to form.

AT A GLANCE
❦ **Plant type** Annual
☼ **Aspect** Full sun
⊚ **Soil type** Compost or growing bags
↓ **Sow seed** Early spring – mid-spring
◎ **Harvest** Late summer – mid-autumn

Which to choose

Heat is an important factor when deciding which chilli to grow, as you need to be able to eat them. However, mild to one person could be hot to another.

Jalapeño is a type of chilli, rather than a variety, and has a moderate to hot flavour. The fruits reach 4cm (1½in) long, and are harvested while green.

'Hungarian Hot Wax' is a mild-tasting variety that also crops well in cooler climates. Green fruits are the mildest but even red fruits are not hot.

'Cherry Bomb' is a prolific variety that produces small rounded fruits that measure 5cm (2in) across. The chillies have a moderate to hot flavour.

Blueberry 'Spartan'

Blueberries

Sumptuously sweet and rich in taste, these berries are easy to grow. The plants also make an attractive feature, with their white spring blossom and autumn tints. Most are self-fertile, meaning you only need one plant to produce a crop, although growing two or more varieties to cross-pollinate each other does give a larger harvest. Keep them well watered and protect the fruit from birds, which will quickly pillage the ripening berries.

Growing advice

Blueberries are acid-loving, so unless you have acid soil, they must be grown in pots. Choose one at least 45cm (18in) across and fill it with lime-free compost.

Container-grown plants should be kept well watered at all times. Feed plants fortnightly from late spring to midsummer with lime-free fertilizer.

AT A GLANCE
- **Plant type** Hardy shrub
- **Height** 1–2m (3–6ft)
- **Spread** 1–1.5m (3–5ft)
- **Aspect** Full sun or partial shade
- **Soil type** Acid, moist, well drained
- **Harvest** Midsummer – early autumn

Sweetcorn 'Sundance'

Growing advice

Sweetcorn has a tall, upright habit. Plant them 45cm (18in) apart in blocks so the pollen from the male flowers falls easily onto the female ones.

When planting out, use a marked cane or a length of wood to help ensure plants are at the right distance apart and spaced evenly.

Harvest the cobs as soon as they are ready to eat by twisting them off at the base. The cobs keep better with their outer leaves left intact.

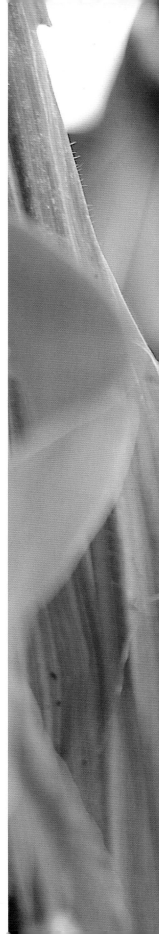

Sweetcorn

Freshly picked homegrown sweetcorn is sweeter and more tender than any you can buy, as its quality declines within hours of picking. Simple to grow, each plant will produce one or two cobs, so plan the number of plants you need accordingly. Seed is best sown under cover into small pots in spring (*see pp.72–73*), to plant out when the risk of frost has passed. Wind spreads sweetcorn pollen, so plant it in blocks, not long rows, to assist pollination. To further help pollination to occur, shake the flower tassels when they begin to open. Keep plants well watered during summer and harvest the cobs when the tassels have turned brown, checking for ripeness first (*see p.199*).

AT A GLANCE
- ❦ **Plant type** Annual
- ☀ **Aspect** Full sun in shelter
- ◉ **Soil type** Fertile and well drained
- ↓ **Sow seed** Mid-spring – late-spring
- ◎ **Harvest** Late summer – early autumn

Agapanthus 'Grand Design'

African lilies

Bearing large heads of trumpet blooms, these perennials, named *Agapanthus*, provide a vibrant display in rich shades of blue and white. They originate from southern Africa, and need plenty of sun and moisture to grow well. There are many varieties to choose but only deciduous forms that die back in winter are reliably hardy; evergreen plants should be brought inside for winter. Ideal for the front of a border, they can also be grown in containers if repotted every 2–3 years. Feed regularly throughout summer for the best display.

Planting partners

African lilies flower over a long period and combine well with many other sun-loving plants. Plant them alongside those with contrasting flower colours.

Sea holly, *Eryngium*, flowers at a similar time to African lilies, with white or blue blooms. The heads dry *in situ* and last into winter.

Cotton lavender, *Santolina*, is a shrubby plant with grey-green leaves and yellow flowers. Use it as a backdrop to African lilies.

AT A GLANCE
- ❧ **Plant type** Hardy/tender perennial
- ⚘ **Height** 60cm–2m (2–6ft)
- ◣ **Spread** 30–60cm (1–2ft)
- ☀ **Aspect** Full sun
- ⊚ **Soil type** Fertile, moist, well drained

Pepper 'Redskin'

Peppers

Known as sweet or bell peppers, these tasty fruits come in a range of colours, shapes, and sizes. The plants need warmth and sunlight to crop well, so are best grown in a greenhouse or outside in a sunny spot. They are also suitable for containers. Grow peppers from seed sown under cover in spring, or buy young plants. Insert canes to support the heavy fruits and keep plants well watered. As soon as flowers appear, apply tomato fertilizer once a fortnight. Peppers can be picked when large enough to use, whether green, yellow, or red.

Growing advice

Pepper have tough fruit stalks that are best cut using secateurs when harvesting. Pulling the fruits off by hand can damage the plant's stems.

AT A GLANCE
- ❀ **Plant type** Annual
- ☀ **Aspect** Full sun
- ◉ **Soil type** Fertile and moist
- ⌄ **Sow seed** Early spring – mid-spring
- ◎ **Harvest** Late summer – early-autumn

Jobs to do:
Summer

Around the garden:
- Plant up bedding displays.
- Mow lawns, and trim hedges and topiary regularly.
- Remove excess weed from ponds.

On the veg patch:
- Net fruit crops against birds.
- Harvest crops as they mature.
- Earth up potatoes as they grow.

In beds and borders:
- Water plants during dry spells.
- Deadhead flowering plants.
- Take cuttings from shrubs.

 Early summer

Summer brings warmer weather and longer days, encouraging all crops and ornamental plants to grow rapidly. Keeping them well watered is essential now, especially for early crops that are soon ready to harvest. Devise a weekly routine to help you keep on top of tasks at this time.

Essential jobs:

* Plant out summer bedding into position (*see p.185*).
* Plant out vegetable seedlings sown directly in seedbeds (*see p.186*).
* Train cordon tomatoes and remove sideshoots (*see p.186*).
* Protect fruiting crops from birds using nets (*see p.187*).
* Cut back spring-flowering bulbs as they die back (*see p.188*).
* Remove the growing tips from broad beans (*see p.188*).
* Harvest crops regularly for a continued supply (*see p.189*).
* Feed fruiting crops with high potash fertilizer (*see p.190*).
* Remove excess weed and algae from ponds (*see p.191*).

Last chance to:

* Sow hardy seeds directly outside (*see pp.70–71*).
* Lift and divide spring-flowering bulbs (*see p.261*).
* Harvest asparagus; now leave the stems to grow all summer.

Continue to:

* Stake perennials and taller bulbs as they grow (*see p.72*).
* Tie climbing crops and ornamentals to their supports.
* Mow the lawn regularly and remove the clippings.
* Trim evergreen shrubs to keep them tidy (*see p.83*).
* Add leafy and twiggy material to the compost heap.

Watch out for:

* Birds feeding on brassica crops and soft fruit – protect plants with netting.

Crops to sow:

Outside: Beetroots, calabrese, carrots, courgettes, Florence fennel, French and runner beans, kale, kohl rabi, lettuces, peas, pumpkins, radishes, spinach, spring cabbages, sprouting broccoli, squashes, summer cauliflowers, swedes, Swiss chard, and turnips.
Under cover: Cucumbers

Crops to plant:

Aubergines, Brussels sprouts, celeriac, celery, chillies, courgettes, cucumbers, French and runner beans, kale, leeks, peppers, sprouting broccoli, and summer cauliflowers.

Harvest now:

Asparagus, beetroots, broad beans, calabrese, carrots, cherries, currants, early potatoes, Florence fennel, garlic, globe artichokes, gooseberries, kohl rabi, lettuces, peas, radishes, rhubarb, spinach, spring cabbages, Swiss chard, strawberries, and turnips.

Plant summer bedding displays

Once the risk of frost has passed it's safe to plant out bedding plants that have been hardened off (*see p.77*) into beds, containers, and hanging baskets. Add some slow-release fertilizer as you plant to help prolong the display, and protect the plants from slug and snail damage.

Training tomatoes into cordons – a single stem grown up a support – is started when the plants are young. Tie the main stem to a vertical support, such as a cane or string, and remove any sideshoots that develop in the leaf joints. Pinching these out prevents the plants wasting energy on unwanted growth and encourages a larger crop.

Vegetable plants raised in seed beds, such as summer cabbages and leeks, can now be lifted and planted into their final position in the vegetable garden. Dig them up carefully to avoid damaging the roots, and water well after planting. Check the seed packet for the correct spacings between plants and rows.

Lightly trimming shrubby herbs, such as rosemary, sage, bay, and thyme improves their shape, and encourages them to bush out and produce flavoursome new growth. Prune rosemary and thyme after flowering but remove the flower buds from sage. If growing bay as topiary, shape it now.

Trim hedges and topiary now and at regular intervals throughout the summer, first making sure that any nesting birds have left before you start. Clip off excess new growth and neaten the hedge or topiary on all sides. Avoid cutting into older growth, especially when trimming conifers, which may not grow back, leaving bald patches.

Citrus plants protected under cover during winter can now be moved outside for summer. Harden them off first (*see p. 77*) to acclimatize them to life outdoors, then give them a sunny, sheltered spot. Water regularly and feed the plants using a special citrus plant fertilizer, which is available from larger garden centres or online.

Netting fruit bushes and trees

to deter birds is best done before the fruit starts to ripen, when it is then easy to spot. Pull the netting taut to prevent birds becoming snagged and pin it down securely at soil level – birds will sneak underneath if not. If you have several plants, erect a simple cage using canes and netting. Trees are harder to protect, but cover what you can with netting or fleece.

Spring-flowering bulbs can be cut to the base once their leaves have yellowed and died. All but tulips can be left undisturbed to flower again next year. Tulips rarely flower reliably for a second year if left in the soil, and should be lifted, dried, and stored. They can then be replanted in late autumn.

Continue providing support for taller perennials and bulbs as they grow to prevent them from collapsing. This is most necessary for those with slender stems, such as penstemons, or large flowers, like lilies. Insert individual garden canes for single stems or use several for clump-forming perennial plants.

Remove the tops from broad bean plants once the first bean pods begin to form, pinching off the top 7cm (3in) of growth. This will encourage an earlier harvest by stopping leafy growth. It also helps to deter blackfly, which commonly infest the soft growing tips, weakening the plants by sucking their sap.

Regular harvests

Harvesting vegetable crops as soon as they are ready allows you to enjoy them at their freshest and best. It also encourages those that crop over a long period, such as beans and peas, to produce larger harvests. Other vegetables that are harvested whole, such as carrots and radishes, can be resown quickly to harvest again a few weeks later.

Shading and ventilating your greenhouse will stop it overheating and drying out in sunny spells, which can damage plants. Open the doors and vents, and fit shading material or apply shade paint to the glass. Soak the floor regularly to increase humidity levels.

Enjoy free new strawberry plants by using bent wire staples to peg the "runners" (*see p.85*) to the soil or the surface of a compost-filled pot buried in the soil. Keep them well watered, and leave them to produce roots and grow on. In late summer, cut the new strawberry plant from its parent and plant it out.

Applying high-potash fertilizer

1 Tomato fertilizer is rich in potash, which encourages plants to flower and produce fruit. Apply it weekly to all fruiting crops, such as tomatoes, peppers, aubergines, and courgettes once their first flowers have appeared.

2 Prepare the tomato fertilizer as directed by the packet and apply it directly to the roots. Avoid splashing the leaves, especially on sunny days, which can be damaged by the feed.

Removing algae and floating weed from ponds helps to keep them healthy by allowing sunlight to reach the water. Use a net to scoop off excess weed and a cane to tease out the algae. Planting aquatic plants (*see pp.126–127*) also helps keep the water clear.

Variegated plants often produce vigorous, plain green shoots, which is known as "reversion". If left to grow, these shoots can take over from the slower-growing coloured growth, spoiling the appearance of your plant. Check variegated plants occasionally and prune out any green stems while young.

Time to prune Shrubs and fruit bushes are pruned now to promote flowers and cropping.

Late spring-flowering shrubs and trees, such as philadelphus and evergreen ceanothus, are pruned after flowering. Cut back flowered shoots to healthy buds, remove any weak growth, and trim back excessively long shoots. On mature plants, very old and woody stems that no longer flower can be cut to the base.

Fruiting currants and gooseberries are pruned now. To prune black currants, remove some of the oldest stems to the base to allow light into the centre. Also remove dead or weak growth. This can also be done in winter. To prune the other currants and gooseberries, cut new sideshoots back to five leaves each. Shorten these again in winter to one bud, and prune out a quarter of the oldest stems to the base, plus any weak or crossing growth.

Midsummer

As summer comes to its peak, many fruit and vegetable crops will be ready to harvest, and ornamental borders will be in full bloom. Watering well, picking produce while fresh, and deadheading spent flowers are all important now to make the most of your earlier hard work.

Essential jobs:

* Thin fruit trees to ensure full-sized fruit (*see p.193*).
* Dry onions, shallots, and garlic on racks (*see p.194*).
* Provide drinking water for garden wildlife (*see p.194*).
* Stop cordon tomatoes by removing the tops (*see p.195*).
* Mulch thirsty crops to help retain moisture (*see p.196*).
* Remove suckers (*see p.196*).
* Cut back excessive new growth on shrubs (*see p.197*).
* Summer-prune established wisteria plants (*see p.197*).
* Prune group 2 clematis after flowering (*see p.197*).
* Prune established cherry and plum trees (*see p.197*).

Last chance to:

* Sow quick-growing crops outside in the soil to harvest before autumn (*see pp.70–71*).

Continue to:

* Weed beds and borders.
* Mow the lawn regularly and keep hedges and topiary trimmed.
* Harvest all crops as soon as they are ready to pick.
* Water all crops regularly during dry spells.
* Cut back flowered perennials for a second flush of colour.
* Water and feed container and basket displays regularly.
* Deadhead flowering plants for a long-lasting display.

Watch out for:

* Blight on tomato plants – treat with fungicide and discard affected fruit.

Crops to sow:

Outside: Beetroots, calabrese, carrots, Florence fennel, French and runner beans, kale, kohl rabi, lettuces, radishes, spinach, spring cabbages, and turnips.

Crops to plant:

Chillies, courgettes, French and runner beans, kale, leeks, maincrop potatoes, peppers, sprouting broccoli, squashes, summer cauliflowers, and winter cabbages and cauliflowers.

Harvest now:

Beetroots, broad beans, calabrese, carrots, cherries, courgettes, cucumbers, currants, early potatoes, Florence fennel, French and runner beans, garlic, gooseberries, kohl rabi, lettuces, onions and shallots, peas, radishes, rhubarb, spinach, spring cabbages, strawberries, summer cauliflowers, summer raspberries, summer squashes, Swiss chard, tomatoes, and turnips.

Thinning fruits

Fruit trees, such as apples, pears, and plums often produce masses of fruitlets, which, if allowed to remain, would result in undersized and unhealthy fruit. Some young fruit naturally falls at this point, known as "June drop", but you may still need to thin them further. Thin the remaining fruits to about 10cm (4in) apart; a little more for cooking apples. To prevent pests and diseases, compost healthy fruits that fall, as well as those you thin out.

Onion, shallot, and garlic plants will soon turn yellow and collapse, meaning the bulbs are ready to harvest. When they have, lift the bulbs and place them on wire racks to dry. Keep them outside if the weather is dry. If not, store them under cover in a dry, airy spot, such as in a shed.

Keeping birdbaths filled during summer is a sure way to attract birds and other wildlife into your garden. Birds and animals can struggle to find enough to drink during hot, dry periods, and birds in particular like to bathe regularly to keep cool. If you can, place your birdbath in the shade so the water evaporates less quickly. Also raise it off the ground to deter stalking cats.

Growing plants from semi-ripe wood cuttings

2 Trim each shoot so that they are around 8–10cm (3–4in) in length, or slightly longer if the plant has large leaves. Remove the main growing tip and trim the base of the stem just below a leaf joint. Nip off the lowest leaves, creating some bare stem to ease into the compost, aiming to leave 4–6 leaves per cutting.

1 Semi-ripe cuttings are so-called because the base of the cutting is woody and the tip soft. Cut off some non-flowering healthy shoots, early in the day when they are full of sap. Place them in a plastic bag filled with a little water to keep them fresh while you collect more cutting material.

Removing faded flowers from plants, "deadheading", keeps them tidy and encourages them to produce new blooms. Pinch off individual flowers with your fingers and cut spent flowerheads back to a bud or a leaf. Leave any plants that have attractive autumn seedheads.

Cordon tomatoes should be "stopped" once they have formed four or five trusses of fruits, or have reached the top of their support. This means removing the top of the main stem to two leaves above the uppermost flower truss. Doing this prevents the plant from wasting energy on unwanted growth and diverts it to producing bigger fruit.

To stop your cauliflower heads discolouring loosely tie some of the plant's own leaves over it to exclude the light. Do this on a dry day to avoid trapping moisture that could rot the head, or "curd", and try not to splash the plant when watering. Occasionally open the leaves up to check for pests and to let the head dry out after rain.

3 Dip the bare base of the cutting into hormone rooting powder, making sure that the cut is properly covered. This should help it to root more quickly. Gently tap the cutting to shake off any excess powder.

4 Insert the cuttings into a pot of moist cutting compost, cover with a clear plastic bag, and position in a cool, light spot, away from direct sun. Keep the compost moist and the cuttings should have rooted by autumn – pull them lightly to check.

Mulching thirsty vegetable crops, such as peas, beans, and courgettes, helps to retain moisture in the soil and reduces how frequently you need to water them – saving you time. Water plants thoroughly first, then apply a thick layer of well-rotted garden compost or manure near their base but not touching the stems. The mulch will also help to suppress emerging weeds.

Many trees and shrubs produce suckers from their base, and, if left, these unwanted, fast-growing shoots will turn into poor quality new plants of little garden use. Use secateurs to help you tear them off (don't cut them) from as close to the base as possible. This will help to ensure they don't resprout.

Fruit attracts wasps that can spoil a crop by eating holes into them, and may sting you if they are disturbed. Avoid this by hanging wasp traps near your plants. These are made by filling jars with sugary liquid and adding a lid with a small hole pierced through. The wasps are lured in by the liquid but can't then escape.

Removing yellowing leaves from pond plants

before they sink or fall into the water helps to keep the pond clean and healthy. Carefully work from the edge of the pond or lay a ladder or platform over the water, ensuring it is secure.

Excessively long new shoots on shrubs

can spoil the overall appearance of the plant. Prune them back in line with other new shoots surrounding it so that the plant maintains a good shape. Rose bushes commonly produce long new stems in summer, known as "water shoots". Cut them back hard to a healthy bud.

Time to prune *Many shrubs, climbers, and fruit bushes can be pruned for shape and flowers.*

Early summer-flowering shrubs,

such as rock roses and weigela, should now be pruned. Cut flowered stems back to healthy buds, remove any dead, damaged, or diseased growth, and prune any very old and woody branches down to the base.

Wisterias are pruned in summer

and winter (*see p.302*). Prune now by cutting back all the wiry new stems so that they have 5–7 pairs of leaves each. This controls the size of the plant, which can be large, and promotes the formation of flower buds for spring.

Group 2 clematis,

such as 'Nelly Moser', that have finished flowering for the first time can be cut back. Prune back some of the shoots that bloomed to healthy buds, which will encourage a second flush of flowers. Prune again in winter (*see p.309*).

Plums, cherries, and apricots

are lightly pruned, and only in summer, to avoid a serious disease called *silver leaf*. Simply remove any dead, dying, or diseased branches, and any that are crossing or rubbing. Aim to create a goblet-shaped tree with an airy, open heart.

Late summer

The season for many plants is beginning to close, and while your borders may be starting to look tired, the vegetable patch will be bountiful as your crops mature. Harvest fruits and vegetables as soon as they are ready, and deadhead flowering plants regularly to prolong their display.

Essential jobs:

* Check sweetcorn for ripeness before harvesting (*see p.199*).
* Collect seeds from annuals and perennials (*see p.200*).
* Cut back this year's growth on lavender bushes (*see p.201*).
* Clean the filter pads fitted to pond pumps (*see p.201*).
* Prune back and tie in summer raspberries after fruiting (*see p.201*).
* Take semi-ripe cuttings of tender perennials (*see p.201*).
* Remove any fallen leaves and plant debris from the surface of ponds.
* Clear away any old growth and debris as plants and crops die back.
* Order spring-flowering bulbs to plant during autumn.

Last chance to:

* Prune the new summer growth on wisterias (*see p.197*).

Continue to:

* Weed beds and borders regularly, including the vegetable patch.
* Mow the lawn regularly.
* Provide water for birds and garden wildlife (*see p.194*).
* Lift and dry late onions, shallots, and garlic bulbs (*see p.194*).
* Water all crops regularly.
* Water and feed container and basket displays regularly.
* Deadhead flowering plants for a long-lasting display.
* Tie in new growth on climbers and wall shrubs.

Crops to sow:

Outside: Carrots, kohl rabi, lettuces, spinach, spring cabbages, Swiss chard, and turnips.

Crops to plant:

Sprouting broccoli and strawberries.

Harvest now:

Aubergines, beetroots, blackberries, blueberries, calabrese, carrots, celery, cherries, chillies, courgettes, cucumbers, currants, early potatoes, Florence fennel, French and runner beans, garlic, kohl rabi, lettuces, onions and shallots, peas, peppers, plums, radishes, spinach, squashes, strawberries, summer and autumn raspberries, summer cabbages and cauliflowers, sweetcorn, Swiss chard, tomatoes, and turnips.

Watch out for:

* Wasps around fruit crops – hang sticky traps near your plants (*see p.196*).

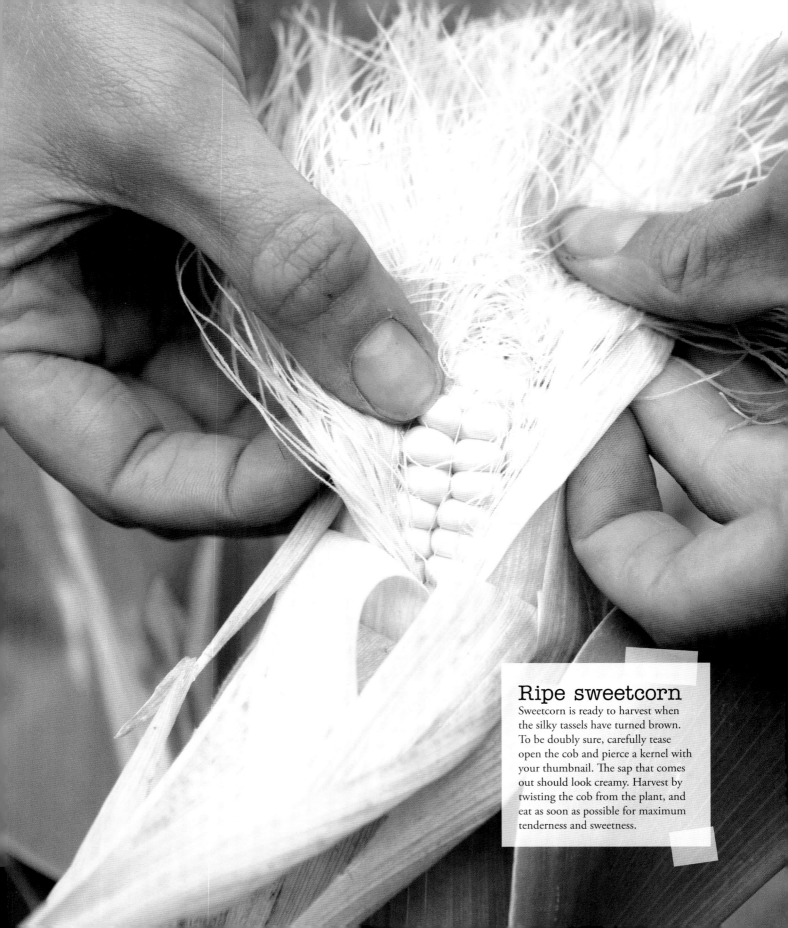

Ripe sweetcorn

Sweetcorn is ready to harvest when
the silky tassels have turned brown.
To be doubly sure, carefully tease
open the cob and pierce a kernel with
your thumbnail. The sap that comes
out should look creamy. Harvest by
twisting the cob from the plant, and
eat as soon as possible for maximum
tenderness and sweetness.

Collect seeds

For free plants next year, collect
seeds from seedheads and pods
from around the garden now.
Choose a dry day and gently crush
the seedheads or pods to free the
seeds, then place them into labelled
envelopes. Store them in a cool, dry
place, ready to sow next year.

Trimming lavender bushes as the flowers fade ensures that the shrubs keep a good shape and don't become leggy with lots of old, woody growth. Remove the flowered stalks and about 2½cm (1in) of green growth below that. Avoid cutting back into older, woodier stems as they often don't resprout.

Pond pump filters can become blocked with algae, plant debris, and silt, which prevents them from working properly. Cleaning them regularly helps to keep pond water clear and healthy for plants and fish. It also ensures water features work as they should. Replace any damaged or missing filters.

Time to prune *Pruning summer raspberry plants now encourages fruiting stems for next year.*

Summer raspberries can be pruned once all the fruit has been harvested. Cut the fruited canes down to ground level, then tie in 6–8 of the new non-fruiting stems per plant along their supports. Prune any surplus new stems down to the base.

Taking cuttings of tender perennials, such as penstemon, fuchsias and geraniums, allows you to keep the young plants under cover and safe from frost, in case the parent plant dies. Look for non-flowering shoots and take semi-ripe wood cuttings (*see pp. 194–195*). Plant them out in late spring.

Autumn

Signs of Autumn

It's the season of mellow fruitfulness – fruits are ripening and vegetables are being harvested. Many annuals and perennials will flower until the first frosts, but the garden is winding down. Annuals are setting seed, perennials are dying back, and deciduous trees and shrubs are losing their leaves – but not before they've put on a spectacular show.

Autumnal equinox

The autumnal equinox occurs around 22–23 September, marking the point at which the Northern Hemisphere begins to tilt away from the Sun, and signalling the start of autumn. At this time, the length of the day and night are roughly the same, just as with the vernal equinox in spring (*see p.17*).

Day length

As the Northern Hemisphere continues to tilt away from the Sun, so the amount of daylight hours received gradually decreases each day until the winter solstice (*see p.277*). This is most pronounced in the north, where the sun rises later and sets earlier than in the south. In Scotland there can be fewer than seven hours of daylight on the shortest days.

Weather

The UK sometimes enjoys a warm period in September and October, referred to as an "Indian summer", with many plants flowering up to the first frosts. But autumn can often bring unsettled weather, storms, and cold snaps as climatic depressions from the Atlantic move over the country. This is therefore a good time to check plant supports in preparation for the wilder weather ahead. The most vibrant displays of autumn leaves occur when a dry summer is followed by a cool, dry, sunny autumn with mild, frost-free nights.

Temperature

The average autumn daytime temperature in this country is around 9°C (48°F), falling as the season progresses. While the days can be relatively mild, frosts become more common at night, which can kill or damage tender plants. "Ground frosts" occur at soil level and are less damaging to plants than "air frosts", when the air around them is below freezing point. The higher up you are, frosts are more likely; if you live in the south, west, or near the coast your garden is less likely to be affected. Many thermometers and weather stations come with a frost alert; alternatively, check your local forecast.

Plant science

Autumn is an important season for plants as they ripen their fruits, disperse seeds, and prepare themselves for winter or, in the case of annuals, die. It is a time of complex and colourful chemistry and biology.

ANNUALS

Even when regularly deadheaded, (*see p.91*) all summer annuals, which includes many vegetable crops, start dying off at this time of year. Exactly what triggers this isn't fully known, but could be related to physical exhaustion, a lack of life-sustaining new growth, plant hormones, or in response to the shortening days. Leaves turn yellow and fall, and stems and roots die back until the plant is completely dead. It lives on through the seeds it produced in summer (unless deadheaded), which in some species can be several thousand.

When annual plants set enough seeds their flowering ceases.

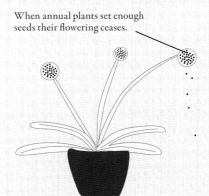

Annual plants die completely and their nutrients are absorbed by the soil.

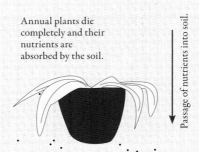

Passage of nutrients into soil.

PERENNIALS

Once flowering finishes, the leafy top growth turns yellow as the valuable nutrients and sugars it contains are drawn into the roots, and converted to starch for storage. The stored starch sustains the plant, which may continue to produce new roots, even though dormant. The shortening days also prompt the development of new shoots and flower buds at the base of the plant, ready to grow in spring. These can occur above or below the soil. If the plant is slightly tender, these should be protected from frost with mulch, such as garden compost, or fleece.

All top growth dies back, often changing colour as it does so.

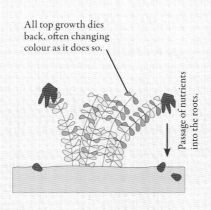

Passage of nutrients into the roots.

Nutrients are stored in the roots, which may continue to grow.

TREES AND SHRUBS

Autumn triggers chlorophyll, the green pigment in plant leaves, to breakdown in deciduous species, leaving red and orange pigments that create the fiery autumnal tints. The leaves fall when ethylene, a gas, builds up inside, causing cells in the stalks to die, allowing them to fall without leaving a wound. Nutrients are drawn deeper into plant tissues, and new growth toughens as cells are reinforced with a chemical called lignin. As fruits mature, bitter-tasting tannins are converted to sugars and their tissues soften to attract dispersing animals and birds.

Leaves change colour as their green pigment breaks down.

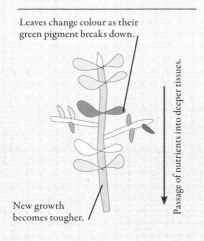

Passage of nutrients into deeper tissues.

New growth becomes tougher.

Fruit tissues soften and sweeten to encourage seed dispersal.

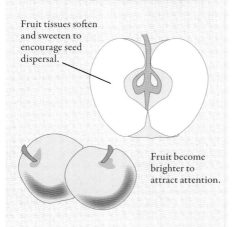

Fruit become brighter to attract attention.

Anemone x *hybrida* 'Hadspen Abundance'

Japanese anemones

With their large simple flowers and wiry stems, these reliable perennials make an elegant addition to the autumn border. Flowering in shades of pink and white, they are ideal for bringing colour to cooler corners of the garden. They prefer soil rich in organic matter, so fork in well-rotted garden compost when planting. Stake taller varieties for support and deadhead spent flowers. Over-sized clumps can be divided (*see p.261*).

Which to choose

The most widely available Japanese anemones that flower in autumn are varieties of *A. hupehensis*, such as 'Hadspen Abundance' (*right*), which grow to 60–90cm (2–3ft) tall, and those of *A.* x *hybrida*, including 'Honorine Jobert' (*below*), reaching 1.2–1.5m (4–5ft). All are reliable and easy to grow.

AT A GLANCE
- ❧ **Plant type** Hardy perennial
- ❦ **Height** 60cm–1.5m (2–5ft)
- ❧ **Spread** 40cm (16in)–indefinite
- ☀ **Aspect** Full sun or dappled shade
- ◎ **Soil type** Fertile and moist

Apple 'Jonagold'
(dessert)

Apples

Apples are one of the most rewarding
fruit trees to grow and there are varieties
to suit all purposes, from sweet dessert
apples to eat fresh, to sharper cooking
types. Whatever variety you choose,
they are all available grafted onto a
range of rootstocks that control their
vigour and size. That means there are
trees suitable for any size of plot, or even
containers. New trees should be watered
regularly for their first year and mulched
annually in spring. Once established, apple
trees need only routine pruning in winter
to encourage healthy plant growth and
a bountiful harvest (*see p.305*).

AT A GLANCE
- ❧ **Plant type** Hardy deciduous tree
- ⚘ **Height** 1.8–6m (6–20ft)
- ⛰ **Spread** 1.8–5m (6–15ft)
- ☼ **Aspect** Full sun
- ◉ **Soil type** Fertile, moist, well drained
- ◎ **Harvest** Early autumn – late autumn

Choosing apples

In order to set fruit, apple flowers must be cross-pollinated with a compatible variety that blooms at the same time, known as a "pollinator". Unless there is one growing nearby, you may need to buy two trees to ensure a crop. Seek advice at the garden centre for the best variety, rootstock, and pollinator.

Garden trees

Apples crop better when grown directly in the soil, and new trees are best planted while dormant (*see p.272*). Unless you have a large garden, consider trees grafted onto dwarfing or semi-dwarfing rootstocks, which limit their mature height to 1.8–4m (6–12ft). If space is limited, consider buying a "family tree" that has two varieties grafted onto the same rootstock, which can eliminate the requirement for a second pollinator tree.

In containers

Apples grow well in containers providing they are kept very well watered, especially when in fruit, and are mulched with garden compost each spring. The best trees for containers are less vigorous varieties grafted onto a semi-dwarfing rootstock, such as M26. Site container-grown trees in a sunny spot, away from strong winds, and repot them every 2–3 years (*see p.268*).

'Spartan'
(dessert)

'Discovery'
(dessert)

'Gravenstein' ....
(dessert)

'Cox's Orange
Pippin' (dessert)

'Howgate Wonder'
(cooking)

Dahlia 'Formby Perfection'

Dahlias

Flowering in an almost endless array of colours, shapes, and sizes, dahlias are simple and rewarding to grow. They range from compact varieties, ideal for pots, to large specimens best in borders. Although they start flowering in summer, their peak display comes in autumn when they continue flowering freely until the first hard frosts. Border dahlias are grown from half-hardy tubers planted in spring. In mild areas they can survive in the soil during winter but, elsewhere, must be lifted and brought under cover. Bedding dahlias are bought as young plants or grown from seed. For the best display, deadhead or pick dahlias regularly, and stake taller varieties.

AT A GLANCE
❧ **Plant type** Half hardy bulbs
⬥ **Height** 45cm–1.5m (18in–5ft)
◣ **Spread** 45–75cm (18–30in)
☀ **Aspect** Full sun, sheltered from wind
◉ **Soil type** Fertile and well drained

Choosing dahlias

Dahlias are highly varied, with flowers ranging from 10–25cm (4–10in) across, and have either green or deep bronze foliage. All enjoy the same growing conditions but large-flowered forms benefit from a sheltered site to stop bad weather damaging their impressive blooms.

D. 'Davenport Honey'

D. 'Glorie van Heemstede'

Dahlia 'Easter Sunday'

D. 'HS First Love'

D. 'Alfred Grille'

Growing advice

Dahlias are versatile, free-flowering plants, suitable for both border and container displays. They are also an excellent source for cut flowers for the home.

Border dahlias are upright, branching plants, and all but the most compact need supporting. These dahlias can be kept from year to year.

Compact bedding dahlias are usually treated like annuals, and are thrown away at the end of the growing season. Buy fresh plants each spring.

Cut border dahlias regularly to ensure a constant supply for indoors but leave enough for a good show in the garden. Bedding types can't be cut.

Sedum spectabile 'Brilliant'

Border sedums

These drought-tolerant perennials are invaluable for the front of an autumn border, and flower in shades of pink and white. Their fleshy, succulent leaves are also attractive and vary in colour from pale grey-green to rich glossy purple, giving interest earlier in the year. They lend themselves to many planting styles, and are magnets for bees and butterflies. Most have attractive seedheads, so don't cut them back in autumn and they'll give winter interest. Sedums do best on soils that aren't too fertile. They need good drainage and don't like wet or heavy soils. Tall varieties may splay out from the middle – cut them back in late spring to help prevent this.

AT A GLANCE
❧ **Plant type** Hardy perennial
↑ **Height** 30–60cm (12–24in)
◀ **Spread** 30–45cm (12–18in)
☀ **Aspect** Full sun
◉ **Soil type** Poor and well drained

Which to choose

Varieties of *Sedum spectabile* (*see left*) all have attractive grey-green foliage, but for even more colour, consider those with rich purple or brightly variegated leaves.

S. erythrostictum **'Mediovariegatum'** has boldly variegated foliage and produces clusters of pale pink flowers. It gives a long season of interest.

S. telephium **Atropurpureum Group** has dark stems and leaves that contrast with its paler flower buds. There are many named varieties to choose.

Chrysanthemum 'Imp'

Chrysanthemums

These tender perennials are highly varied, bearing flowers in a diverse range of shapes and colours. Most are tall, ideal for the back of borders, and are excellent for cutting. New plants are best bought each spring or grown from cuttings taken from plants brought inside for winter. Shortly after planting, pinch out the tips to encourage more flower shoots, and provide support for taller varieties. When frosts kill the flowers, cut the stems back and protect the crown with thick mulch. In colder areas, lift the plants and move them to a cold frame or an unheated greenhouse until spring.

Which to choose

Double-flowered chrysanthemums, such as 'Membury' (*above*), are the most dramatic, and can be fully round or flattened in shape.

Single-flowered varieties, like 'Talbot Jo' (*above*), have simpler, weather-resistant blooms that are ideal for exposed plots.

AT A GLANCE
- ✤ **Plant type** Half hardy perennial
- ✿ **Height** 30cm–1.5m (1–5ft)
- ✿ **Spread** 60–100cm (2–3ft)
- ☼ **Aspect** Full sun
- ◉ **Soil type** Fertile and well drained

Aster amellus 'Blue King'

Autumn asters

Coming into bloom as other perennials are dying back, autumn-flowering asters breathe new life into borders. Plant them in drifts in a mix of varieties for an easy-to-grow medley of pink, blue, white, and purple daisy blooms. Upright, branching plants, they are ideal for a mid-border position. Taller forms require staking, especially if grown in exposed sites. Deadhead plants regularly and water them well during dry periods to prevent powdery mildew developing on the leaves. Established clumps can be lifted and divided if congested to restore their vigour (*see p.261*).

AT A GLANCE
- ❦ **Plant type** Hardy perennial
- ♠ **Height** 75cm–1.5m (30–60in)
- 🍃 **Spread** 45–90cm (18–36in)
- ☼ **Aspect** Full sun or light shade
- ☺ **Soil type** Moist but well drained

Which to choose

When choosing asters to grow for autumn colour, look out for varieties of *A. amellus*, *A. novae-angliae*, and *A. novi-belgii*.

Dome-forming *Aster amellus* (*left*) forms a spreading clump of colour, ideal for the front of a border. *A. novae-angliae* (*above*) is taller with an upright habit; plant it mid-border.

Michaelmas daisy, *A. novi-belgii* (*above*), is similar to *A. novae-angliae*, and can be used in the same way in the garden. There are many varieties and colours to choose from.

Grasses for autumn
Seedheads

Ornamental grasses are invaluable for adding structure, movement, and texture to a border, especially if planted *en masse*. At their peak in autumn, when their seedheads turn buff or silver, they often persist well into winter.

1 *Cortaderia selloana* Evergreen pampas grass is a large plant, ideal for island beds and borders.
🌱 2.5m (8ft) ↔ 1.5m (5ft)

2 *Panicum virgatum* This bears billowing clouds of tiny flowers that sway gently in the wind.
🌱 1.5m (5ft) ↔ 1m (3ft)

3 *Miscanthus sinensis* Tall and clump-forming, this grass is ideal for summer screening, with colourful variegated forms to grow.
🌱 1.8m (6ft) ↔ 1.2m (4ft)

4 *Eragrostis curvula* Delicate and graceful, this large grass bears arching panicles of flowers.
🌱 1.2m (4ft) ↔ 1.2m (4ft)

5 *Lagurus ovatus* Known as hare's tails, this is a compact annual grass to grow from seed.
🌱 50cm (20in) ↔ 50cm (20in)

6 *Calamagrostis brachytricha* A large plant, it flowers in late summer and turns gold in autumn.
🌱 1.2m (4ft) ↔ 1m (3ft)

7 *Chasmanthium latifolium* This broad-leaved grass has unusual, diamond-shaped flowers that are excellent for drying.
🌱 1m (3ft) ↔ 60cm (2ft)

8 *Pennisetum setaceum* Known as fountain grass, it bears long, tactile blooms. Protect it in winter.
🌱 1m (3ft) ↔ 60cm (2ft)

9 *Briza maxima* Annual quaking grass has flowerheads that quiver in the breeze. It self-seeds readily.
🌱 50cm (20in) ↔ 30cm (12in)

10 *Stipa calamagrostis* This grass has narrow, arching leaves, topped by silvery flowerheads that turn beige during autumn.
🌱 1m (3ft) ↔ 1.2m (4ft)

Pear 'Le Lectier'
(dessert)

Pears

Pears taste amazing when perfectly ripe and growing your own is the best way to enjoy them in peak condition. They are grown in a similar way to apples (*see pp.210–213*), although need a warmer, more sheltered site, as their early blossom can be damaged by frost. There are many varieties to choose, either dessert or cooking types, which are available on dwarfing and semi-dwarfing rootstocks. Like apples, pear flowers must be pollinated by another variety to set fruit, so you may need to plant more than one to get a crop. Easy to grow, new trees should be watered regularly in their first year, while established specimens should be mulched with garden compost each spring and pruned in winter (*see p.305*).

AT A GLANCE
- ❦ **Plant type** Hardy deciduous tree
- ❦ **Height** 3.5–6m (11–20ft)
- ❦ **Spread** 3–4m (10–12ft)
- ❦ **Aspect** Full sun in shelter
- ☺ **Soil type** Fertile, moist, well drained
- ◎ **Harvest** Early autumn – mid-autumn

....

Which to choose

Most pears can be picked and eaten straight from the tree, but there are cooking varieties, such as 'Catillac'. As a compromise, consider dual-purpose pears that can be cooked or enjoyed fresh.

'**Williams' Bon Chrétien**' is a dual-purpose pear with a musky flavour. It crops in early autumn, bearing large pale green fruit that stores well. The tree tolerates some shade.

'**Gorham**' is a dessert pear with a sweet, mellow flavour. The small- to medium-sized fruits have a yellow-green hue in early autumn, and are covered with light brown russet.

'**Louise Bonne Jersey**' fruits in mid-autumn, producing medium-sized dessert pears with soft, juicy flesh. Its blossom is frost-resistant but the tree still requires a sheltered site.

Pumpkin 'Jack of all Trades'

Pumpkins

These large fruits are perhaps most commonly thought of as Halloween decorations but they are also delicious to eat, especially in soups and pies. They are large, sprawling plants that are very simple to grow, as long as you have rich soil and ample space. Sow seeds on their sides into individual pots under cover during mid-spring, or directly where they are to grow in early summer. Keep the plants well watered all summer and start feeding with tomato fertilizer fortnightly once the fruits appear. For large pumpkins, thin the fruits to one per plant; thin to 3–4 for smaller fruits.

Growing advice

In addition to how they are grown, pumpkin size depends on variety. For the largest fruits, try 'Dills Atlantic Giant'.

To prevent pumpkins rotting as they grow, and to keep their skins clean, place the developing fruits on bricks or blocks to raise them off the damp soil surface.

AT A GLANCE
- ❦ **Plant type** Annual
- ☀ **Aspect** Full sun
- ◉ **Soil type** Fertile and moist
- ↓ **Sow seed** Mid-spring – early summer
- ◎ **Harvest** Early autumn – mid-autumn

Nerines

With their vibrant trumpet-like flowers, nerines radiate colour and bring a touch of exoticism to the autumn garden. The plants look delicate but are surprisingly robust and flower for several weeks. To grow well, they need sun, shelter, and good drainage, and thrive when planted at the base of a warm wall. Nerines form large, dense clumps over time and resent being disturbed, so shouldn't be lifted and divided often. In colder areas, bring pot-grown plants indoors for winter.

Which to choose

Although nerines originate from South Africa, *N. bowdenii* and its varieties are fully hardy. All other species require winter protection.

N. x ***bowdenii*** (*right*) flowers late in the season. For earlier, and equally flamoyant colour, plant daylilies (*Hemerocallis, above*) and red hot pokers (*Kniphofia*), which enjoy similar conditions.

AT A GLANCE
- ❦ **Plant type** Hardy/half hardy bulb
- ⚘ **Height** 45–60cm (18–24in)
- ◭ **Spread** 45–60cm (18–24in)
- ☼ **Aspect** Full sun
- ◉ **Soil type** Moist and well drained

Make: Instant topiary

Topiary adds real character to any garden, and can be whatever size and shape you choose. Bought examples can be expensive, and starting from scratch takes years, but you can achieve a similar effect using a pre-shaped wire topiary frame and ivy.

YOU WILL NEED
★ Materials:
Pre-shaped wire topiary frame
Suitably-sized container
Soil-based compost
Young ivy plants
Wire pegs
Soft string

1 Choose a container large enough for the topiary frame and for the number of ivy plants you are using. Be sure the pot has drainage holes. Space out the ivy, plant into soil-based compost, and remove any canes.

2 Trail the stems of your ivy plants over the edge of the pot. Place the topiary frame on the container, ensuring it is vertical and positioned centrally. Use wire pegs pushed into the compost to hold it in place.

4 Cover the frame so that the ivy stems are evenly spaced all the way around, then pinch out their top growing tips. This will cause the plants to produce sideshoots that you can later train to fill in any gaps.

3 Take the first ivy stem and wrap it around the frame to judge how much coverage each plant gives. The stems can either be attached to the frame by tying them in place with soft garden string or by carefully weaving them through the wire frame.

5 Water the container well and place it in a sheltered position until the plants establish. Keep it well watered thereafter and tie new stems regularly to maintain the shape. Mulch with compost in spring.

Chusquea culeou

Bamboos

Many evergreen bamboos have attractive and colourful stems, which can best be seen in autumn when neighbouring plants die back. The most dramatic canes belong to tall, clump-forming bamboos, which can be planted as screens, informal hedges, or focal points. Unlike spreading types, these bamboos are not invasive – their dense clumps simply becoming broader over time. Once established, bamboos need little routine care, other than removing dead canes occasionally. To see their canes more clearly, remove some of the lower leaves. Although hardy, bamboos prefer a sheltered position, away from damaging cold winds.

AT A GLANCE
- ❦ **Plant type** Hardy grass
- ⚘ **Height** 2–10m (6–30ft)
- 🍂 **Spread** 2–3m (6–9ft)
- ☀ **Aspect** Full sun or partial shade
- ◉ **Soil type** Moist but well drained

Which to choose

Tall and elegant, *Chusquea culeou* (*left*) forms a dense clump of attractive, glossy green canes with a banded appearance. Its foliage resembles bottlebrushes.

Yellow groove bamboo, *Phyllostachys aureosulcata* f. *aureocaulis,* is a colourful choice for the back of a border. Spent canes can be used in the garden.

Black bamboo, *Phyllostachys nigra*, produces dark green canes that take 2–3 years to mature to glossy black. It is a good choice for oriental-style gardens.

Celeriac 'Monarch'

Celeriac

Related to celery and with a similar taste, this unusual vegetable is steadily acquiring gourmet status. Although it looks like a root crop, the edible part is the plump, knobbly stem from which the leaves sprout. Start the seeds under cover in early spring (*see pp.72–73*), and plant them out in early summer, 45cm (18in) apart. Cold spells can make them "bolt" – to flower suddenly – so cover them with fleece at first. Keep plants well watered and don't worry if they appear to grow slowly, as they put on a growth spurt in autumn. Harvest celeriac between mid-autumn and early spring.

Growing advice

Once planted out, celeriac needs little routine care other than regular watering. The crop can become tough if the plants dry out in summer.

In addition to the plump main stem at the base of the plant, the leaves and fleshy leaf stalks are also edible, and have a strong celery-like flavour. Pick individual leaves sparingly to flavour soups.

AT A GLANCE
- ❦ **Plant type** Hardy biennial
- ☼ **Aspect** Full sun
- ◉ **Soil type** Fertile, moist, well drained
- ↓ **Sow seed** Early spring – late autumn
- ◎ **Harvest** Late spring – winter

Brussels sprouts 'Trafalgar'

Brussels sprouts

Named after the city where they were first discovered, this essential winter crop can span the first to the last frosts. In fact, frost plays a useful role in their flavour, making them taste sweeter. Brussels sprouts are easy to grow but need plenty of space, so are best for larger plots. Sow seed in early to late spring into a seedbed, before transplanting them to their final positions in late spring or early summer, 60cm (24in) apart. Cover young plants with netting to protect them against pigeon attacks. Brussels sprouts can become top-heavy and may topple over, so insert canes or mound soil around their bases to keep them upright.

AT A GLANCE
❦ **Plant type** Hardy biennial
☀ **Aspect** Full sun
◉ **Soil type** Rich, moist, and fertile
↓ **Sow seed** Early spring – late spring
◎ **Harvest** Early autumn – early spring

Growing advice

Once in their final growing positions, keep plants well watered. To encourage a larger crop, feed in autumn with a high-nitrogen fertilizer.

Harvest Brussels sprouts as you need to from the base of the plant upwards, snapping them off downwards. Surplus sprouts can be frozen.

Sprout tops, the leafy crown on top of the stem, make an excellent cabbage-like crop. Cut it once the sprouts have been picked.

Plants for Autumn foliage

Every garden needs deciduous trees, shrubs, or climbers that develop spectacular autumn leaf colour. Whether you have a large or small plot, there are plenty of suitable plants to choose from.

1 Betula alleghaniensis Known as the yellow birch, the leaves of this tree turn rich buttery yellow.
♠ 12m (40ft) 🔻 8m (25ft)

2 Parthenocissus tricuspidata A fast-growing climber, Boston ivy turns bright crimson in autumn. Best for walls, it needs ample space.
♠ 12m (40ft) 🔻 8m (25ft)

3 Liquidambar styraciflua A great tree for autumn colour, its aromatic leaves pass through a riot of shades before they fall.
♠ 25m (80ft) 🔻 12m (40ft)

4 Amelanchier lamarckii An all-season tree with spring blossom, summer fruit, and autumn colour.
♠ 1.2m (4ft) 🔻 1.2m (4ft)

5 Prunus sargentii A flowering spring cherry, its leaves turn bright orange and red in autumn.
♠ 20m (70ft) 🔻 15m (50ft)

6 Cornus kousa Grown for its spring flowers, the leaves of this small tree turn crimson in autumn.
♠ 7m (22ft) 🔻 5m (15ft)

7 Rhus typhina 'Dissecta' The finely cut leaves of this large shrub turn vivid yellow and red.
♠ 2m (6ft) 🔻 3m (10ft)

8 Hydrangea quercifolia This shrub flowers in summer, and its oak-like leaves turn red in autumn.
♠ 2m (6ft) 🔻 2.5m (8ft)

9 Parrotia persica In autumn, each leaf on this stunning tree appears to be a different shade of either red, orange, yellow, or purple.
♠ 8m (25ft) 🔻 10m (30ft)

10 Euonymus alatus This spindle tree comes into its own during autumn, when its green foliage turns dazzling crimson.
♠ 2m (6ft) 🔻 3m (10ft)

Acer palmatum 'Trompenburg'

Maples

Graceful in spring and summer, maples become an inferno of colour as their leaves fall in autumn. Botanically named *Acer*, they range from cascading shrubs to stately trees, and all are easy to grow. New acers are best planted while dormant (*see p.272*) so they have time to establish a little before spring. All are fully hardy but those with small or dissected foliage can be damaged by drying winds in summer, so are best given sheltered positions. Maples don't require regular pruning but over-sized trees can be cut back hard in autumn or winter.

AT A GLANCE
❧ **Plant type** Hardy deciduous trees/shrubs
🌲 **Height** 2.5–20m (8–70ft)
🍃 **Spread** 2.5–20m (8–70ft)
☀ **Aspect** Full sun or partial shade
◉ **Soil type** Fertile, moist, well drained

Growing advice

In addition to their vivid autumnal tints, there are many acers you can grow that also provide welcome interest at other times of year.

The spring foliage of many acers, such as *A. pseudoplatanus* 'Brilliantissimum' (*above*), is richly coloured until it fades in midsummer.

Summer to autumn is when the intricately cut foliage of Japanese maples, *A. palmatum*, are at their most beautiful and textural.

The bare, leafless stems of some acers, such as *A. pensylvanicum* 'Erythrocladum' (*above*), seem to glow in soft winter light.

Choosing maples

This is a large and varied group of trees and all but the Japanese maples, *Acer palmatum*, are quick growing. Most develop stunning autumnal tints, although for maximum interest, consider those that also have deep bronze or brightly variegated leaves in summer. These are leafy trees and form large, dense canopies in time, so bear in mind the shade they'll cast when deciding which to grow.

Acer cappadocicum
'Aureum'

A. rubrum

A. platanoides
'Crimson Sentry'

A. negundo
'Flamingo'

A. platanoides
'Drummondii'

A. palmatum

Ideal for pots

Slow-growing Japanese maples,
A. palmatum (*right*), are the best for
containers, with both weeping and
upright forms, plus those with coloured
and dissected leaves. Plant into a large
container filled with soil-based compost,
and position it in a sheltered spot away
from the midday sun. Water regularly
throughout summer and mulch with
garden compost during early spring.

Border trees

In addition to growing in containers,
A. palmatum and its varieties are also
ideal for planting in borders. Other
good choices include *A. negundo*
'Flamingo', which has variegated leaves
(*see left*), and *A. shirasawanum* 'Aureum',
with its bright yellow-green summer
foliage. Both then also develop fiery
tints in autumn before their leaves fall.

Large gardens

Many maples can grow very large and
make excellent specimen trees in bigger
gardens. More colourful choices include
A. platanoides 'Drummondii', which
has cream-variegated foliage (see *left*),
and *A. cappadocicum* 'Aureum', which
has acid yellow young leaves in spring
(*see far left*) that mellow during summer.
Both also develop rich autumnal tints.

Cyclamen hederifolium

Hardy cyclamen

Blooming before their leaves appear, autumn-flowering cyclamen, *C. hederifolium*, provides weeks of colour in shades of pink or white. They are ideal for planting on rockeries or beneath deciduous shrubs, where they freely bloom below the disappearing canopy. The marbled leaves give interest through winter and die back in spring. Plant them while in growth and deadhead the spent blooms unless you want them to self-seed (*see below*). These bulbs need little care. Once planted, simply mulch them in spring with garden compost.

Growing advice

If left undisturbed and allowed to set seed, *C. hederifolium* slowly forms attractive colonies. The plants may also naturally hybridize with each other, resulting in a carpet of flowers in varying shades of pink and white.

AT A GLANCE
- ❦ **Plant type** Hardy bulb
- ⚑ **Height** 10–15cm (4–6in)
- ♣ **Spread** 15–20cm (6–8in)
- ☼ **Aspect** Dappled shade
- ◉ **Soil type** Well drained and humus-rich

Squash 'Turk's Turban'

Winter squashes

So-named because they keep well during winter, these squashes need a couple of months in storage to develop their nutty flavour. Sow seeds under cover in mid-spring to plant out later, or sow directly in the soil in early summer. These large, trailing plants need rich soil, so dig in garden compost before planting. Keep them well watered and feed with tomato fertilizer when the first fruits begin to swell. Harvest the fruits in late summer when they reach full size, leaving some of the stalk attached. Store them in an airy, frost-free place.

AT A GLANCE
- **Plant type** Annual
- **Aspect** Full sun
- **Soil type** Fertile and moist
- **Sow seed** Mid-spring – midsummer
- **Harvest** Late-summer – early autumn

Which to choose

Winter squashes come in a variety of shapes, sizes, and colours. All have firm flesh that develops a mild, nutty flavour over time.

Crown prince squashes have pale blue-grey skins and bright orange flesh. If thinned, the largest fruits can weigh up to 4kg (9lb) each.

Acorn Squashes have a green or yellow skin and orange flesh, and reach up to 20cm (8in) long. Varieties include 'Honey Bear'.

Butternut squashes are the most widely grown and have pale orange skins with darker flesh. The fruits reach 25cm (10in) long.

Leek 'Blue Solaise'

Leeks

With their sweet, mild, onion-like taste, leeks are a staple crop from autumn to spring, and can be left in the soil until needed. They are hungry plants, so prepare the soil the previous autumn or winter by digging in well rotted garden compost. Seed can be sown under cover or outside, ready to plant out from late spring when the seedlings are pencil-thick. Keep the plants well watered in summer, and remove any weeds, as leeks hate competition. Baby leeks can be harvested in late summer.

Growing advice

Leek stems are made sweeter by excluding light. To do this, seedlings are planted deeply (see below). Soil can also be piled around adult plants.

To plant leek seedlings, trim their roots, then make narrow holes 15cm (6in) deep, spaced 20–30cm (8–12in) apart. Drop in the leeks and trickle water into the holes so they partially backfill with soil.

AT A GLANCE
- ❋ **Plant type** Hardy biennial
- ☼ **Aspect** Full sun
- ⊙ **Soil type** Fertile, moist, well drained
- ↓ **Sow seed** Early spring – late spring
- ◎ **Harvest** Autumn – mid-spring

Shrubs for
Autumn berries

In addition to fiery foliage, autumn is the season for decorative berries and fruits, which can provide colour for many months. They are also an essential source of food for wildlife in winter, giving even more reason to grow them.

1 ***Berberis thunbergii*** This spiky deciduous shrub bears glossy, long-lasting fruit in autumn.
🌱 1m (3ft) ◣ 2.5m (8ft)

2 ***Symphoricarpos* x *doorenbosii*** A large deciduous shrub, it has small white flowers in late summer, followed by plump white berries.
🌱 2m (6ft) ◣ 4m (12ft)

3 ***Rosa rugosa*** This tough shrub rose has scented summer flowers followed by glossy round red hips.
🌱 1.5m (5ft) ◣ 1.5m (5ft)

4 ***Aronia* x *prunifolia* 'Brilliant'** The white flowers of this shrub give way in autumn to red and black berries, and wine-red foliage.
🌱 2m (6ft) ◣ 3m (10ft)

5 ***Cornus kousa*** Mature shrubs bear strawberry-like fruits in summer, which turn red in autumn.
🌱 7m (22ft) ◣ 5m (15ft)

6 ***Cotoneaster horizontalis*** Best planted against a wall, this deciduous shrub is smothered with small red berries during autumn.
🌱 1m (3ft) ◣ 1.5m (5ft)

7 ***Cotoneaster salicifolius*** This large arching evergreen shrub bears abundant glossy red berries.
🌱 5m (15ft) ◣ 5m (15ft)

8 ***Pyracantha* 'Orange Glow'** This deciduous shrub has white flowers followed by orange fruit.
🌱 3m (10ft) ◣ 3m (10ft)

9 ***Euonymus europaeus*** The bold autumn leaves of this deciduous shrub accompany unusual red fruits.
🌱 3m (10ft) ◣ 2.5m (8ft)

10 ***Callicarpa dichotoma*** Known as beauty berry, this deciduous shrub has striking glossy purple fruits that persist into winter.
🌱 1.2m (4ft) ◣ 1.2m (4ft)

Jobs to do:
Autumn

Around the garden:
- Renovate lawns before winter.
- Protect tender plants from frost.
- Regularly remove fallen leaves.

On the veg patch:
- Harvest fruit and vegetable crops.
- Prepare the soil ready for spring
  as beds become empty.

In beds and borders:
- Plant new trees, shrubs, and
  perennials.
- Divide congested perennials.
- Plant spring-flowering bulbs.

Early Autumn

This is a productive time in the garden with fruit trees and late vegetables coming into full harvest, so take time to pick, cut, or pull your maturing crops regularly. As plants die back, clear away and compost any spent growth to help control pests and diseases for next year.

Essential jobs:

* Order bare-root trees, shrubs, and fruit plants (*see p.258*).
* Plant up containers with trees and shrubs (*see pp.258–259*).
* Lift tender bulbs and bring them under cover (*see p.259*).
* Cut back perennials as their stems die off (*see p.259*).
* Plant spring-flowering bulbs, except tulips (*see p.260*).
* Clear away spent annual bedding displays (*see p.261*).
* Divide overgrown perennials and congested bulbs (*see p.261*).
* Renovate your lawn in time for winter (*see p.262*).
* Dry chillies (*see p.263*).
* Prepare autumn bedding displays and containers (*see p.263*).

Last chance to:

* Sow new lawns from seed (*see p.81*).
* Trim and tidy evergreen shrubs and hedges (*see p.83*).

Continue to:

* Prune out reverted growth on variegated plants (*see p.191*).
* Deadhead flowering plants to prolong the display.
* Water plants growing in containers during dry spells.
* Feed bedding plants growing in containers and baskets.
* Weed beds, borders, and vegetable patches.
* Remove and compost plant debris from around the garden.

Crops to sow:

Outside: Lettuces and Swiss chard (under cloches).

Crops to plant:

Strawberries.

Harvest now:

Apples, aubergines, autumn raspberries, beetroots, blackberries, blueberries, Brussels sprouts, calabrese, carrots, celery, cherries, chillies, courgettes, cucumbers, Florence fennel, French and runner beans, kohl rabi, leeks, lettuces, maincrop potatoes, onions and shallots, pears, peas, peppers, plums, pumpkins, radishes, spinach, squashes, strawberries, summer cabbages and cauliflowers, swedes, sweetcorn, Swiss chard, and turnips.

Watch out for:

* Powdery mildew on fruit and vegetables – water well and pinch off infected leaves.

Pumpkin season

Pumpkins are ready to harvest when their skins are hard and they sound hollow when tapped. Cut the fruit off with its stalk (don't use it as a handle – it can damage the fruit) and raise the fruit off the damp soil onto blocks. Leave the fruit in the sun for ten days to "cure" before carving or storing.

Many spring-flowering bulbs, such as crocus and daffodils, can be planted in lawns and left to naturalize over many years. Scatter the bulbs randomly and plant them where they fall. Use a bulb planter to make holes in the turf, plant the bulb at three times its depth, then replace the turf plug.

Buying bare-root trees and shrubs gives you the best choice, especially when choosing fruit varieties. Order them now from local and mail-order nurseries for the healthiest plants. Plant them as soon as soon as you receive them in the same way as for container-grown trees and shrubs (*see p.272*).

Planting trees and shrubs in containers

1 Choose a container that provides enough space for your tree or shrub to grow for a number of years, making sure it has drainage holes in the bottom. As a guide, use the plant's original pot when choosing the right size.

2 Cover the drainage holes with stones to ensure water drains through them freely, then fill the pot with compost. Use the old pot as a guide when adding the compost.

Tender bulbs can be lifted and stored under cover once their top growth has died back. Bulbs like begonias and gladioli should be cleaned of soil and stored wrapped in dry, airy material, such as straw. Leave dahlias until they have been frosted and their leaves blackened, then cut the stems down, lift the tubers, and store them in trays of dry compost.

Remove baby figs that are any larger than pea-size as they won't develop any further at this time of year and will rot away. Only small figlets survive the winter, and then develop the following summer to reach maturity. To help ensure their survival, cover the figlets with garden fleece in late autumn to protect them from frost.

Cutting back spent perennials helps keep your beds and borders tidy, and removes hiding places for pests and diseases. However, leave those with attractive seedheads, such as sedums (*see pp.218–219*), as these will give the garden interest in winter and will provide food for birds. Don't cut back penstemons – their woody growth helps to protect them from frost.

3 Remove the pot guide carefully to prevent the compost collapsing into the planting hole you have made.

4 Place the tree or shrub into the planting hole and add or remove compost so that the top of the rootball sits 5cm (2in) below the rim of the container, and is level with the surrounding compost. Gently firm the plant in with your hands and water it thoroughly.

Clearing away plant debris as ornamentals and vegetable crops begin to die back is an effective way to deter the build-up of pests and diseases by denying them somewhere to lurk during winter. It also keeps the garden tidy. All but diseased material can be composted, which should be burned or discarded at a refuse centre.

To harvest apples at their best, hold the fruit in your hand and gently twist. It should come away easily with its stalk. Pears should be firm and plump, and their skin may change colour. They can be picked slightly underripe as they continue to ripen after picking.

Hardy perennial vegetables, such as asparagus, rhubarb, and globe artichokes, should be cut back at this time. Prune yellowed asparagus foliage down to ground level. Cut back old rhubarb stalks to leave the buds exposed to cold over winter. Remove the stems of globe artichokes and cover with a thick mulch of straw or bark to protect the crown.

Spring-flowering bulbs are best bought early for the largest choice and healthiest bulbs. Plant them as soon as you can at a depth of three times the height of the bulb. If you can't plant them straight away, store bulbs somewhere that is cool, dark, and well-ventilated. Tulips are best planted in late autumn to avoid the disease, *tulip fire* (see p.40).

Dividing perennials and bulbs

Growing new plants from hardwood cuttings

Cut woody stems 15–30cm (6–12in) long and remove the soft top growth, cutting above a bud at an angle. Dip the base into hormone rooting powder and plant them two-thirds deep into pots of compost outdoors. They will root and be ready to plant out next autumn – check for rooting by pulling gently.

Summer bedding plants will be past their best and should be removed. If you haven't already saved seed from annuals, such as cornflower or marigold, it's not too late (*see p.200*). Dig up the spent plants and put them on the compost heap, along with any other plant debris.

1 Lift the perennial or clump of bulbs from the soil with a garden fork or spade, taking care not to damage the roots. Especially large clumps may need to be lifted in sections so they are easier to lift and handle. Shake off the excess soil so you can see the rootball clearly.

2 Divide the clump into smaller sections, each with healthy bulbs, buds, or shoots. Most bulbs, such as lilies, can usually be split using your hands but established perennials may need prizing apart using two garden forks or spades held back-to-back.

3 Check each of the divisions for signs of weak, diseased, or dead growth, and also inspect the roots. When you divide clumps of bulbs, such as nerines, discard the oldest bulbs from the centre that no longer flower, and only keep the young, healthy ones near the outside.

4 Replant the divided perennials and bulbs as soon as possible, at the same depth as the original clump. Prepare a planting hole, spread out the roots well, and backfill with soil. Firm the plants in and water well. Continue to water regularly as they re-establish.

Renovating your lawn

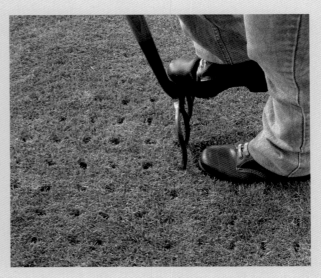

1 Grass clippings, moss, and plant debris regularly builds up in lawns, which stifles growth and encourages moss and disease. Remove it each year using a spring-tine rake (*above*) and put it in the compost heap. This may leave your lawn looking messy at first but it will soon recover.

2 Aerating the lawn by spiking it all over improves drainage and airflow, which encourages healthy growth and helps to control moss. Using a garden fork, wiggling it back and forwards, pierce holes at 15cm (6in) intervals. Focus on areas that are heavily used or where the ground is compacted.

3 "Top-dressing" is a sand and soil mixture bought from garden centres that is applied to lawns after aerating them. Spread over the lawn, it improves surface drainage, which promotes lawn health and helps to control moss. Apply top-dressing at the rate specified on the bag.

4 Using a stiff brush or rake, spread the top-dressing evenly over the lawn, working it into the fork holes. More can be added if necessary to even out shallow dips and small hollows to create a level surface. Hose the lawn with a fine spray to help settle the top-dressing unless it rains soon.

Winter and spring bedding plants can be planted now for colourful displays. Choose suitable containers with plenty of drainage holes and part-fill them with peat-based compost. Add some spring-flowering bulbs, like tulips and dwarf daffodils, cover with compost, then plant a mix of bedding plants on top for a long-lasting show. Position the container in a sheltered site if possible.

Spring cabbages that were sown outside in late summer can be transplanted into their final positions now. Refer to the spacings given on the seed packet and plant them out accordingly. Water in and cover immediately with fine plastic netting, pulled taut, to avoid attacks from pigeons.

Maincrop potatoes are ready to lift when their leafy top growth turns yellow. Cut the growth back, wait for about ten days, then carefully dig up the potatoes using a garden fork. Leave the tubers to dry on the soil for a few hours (inside if the weather is wet) before storing them under cover in paper sacks.

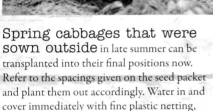

Drying chillies to store is a great way to make use of a surplus crop, and allows you to use them throughout the year. Thread the fresh chillies onto strings and hang them in a warm, well ventilated spot under cover until the skins are dry, dark, and crisp. You can then use them as required.

Mid-autumn

Although the days are still warm, the nights will begin to get colder, so now is the period to start protecting tender plants from frost by bringing them under cover or protecting them outside. Clearing fallen leaves is also an important task now, as they can smother lawns and plants if left.

Essential jobs:

❋ Cut and dry attractive seedheads for indoor displays (*see p.265*).
❋ Rake fallen leaves from all around the garden (*see p.266*).
❋ Plant new deciduous hedges, such as beech (*see p.266*).
❋ Leave winter habitat areas for garden wildlife (*see p.267*).
❋ Insulate greenhouses against frost using bubble plastic (*see p.267*).
❋ Cut back climbing roses to avoid wind damage (*see p.267*).
❋ Prepare the soil in empty beds for spring (*see p.268*).
❋ Protect tender plants outside against frost (*see p.268*).
❋ Move smaller tender plants, such as those in containers, under cover for winter (*see p.269*).

Last chance to:

❋ Lift tender bulbs before the hard frosts arrive (*see p.259*).
❋ Finish harvesting tender crops, such as tomatoes, grown outside.

Continue to:

❋ Plant spring-flowering bulbs, except tulips (*see p.260*).
❋ Take hardwood cuttings from hardy shrubs (*see p.261*).
❋ Cut back perennials as they continue to die back.
❋ Remove fallen leaves and plant debris floating on ponds.
❋ Order new bare-root trees and shrubs to plant soon.
❋ Put fresh water out for birds and other garden wildlife daily.

Watch out for:

❋ Coral spot fungus on trees and shrubs – prune out all affected growth.

Crops to sow:

Under cover: Broad beans and winter lettuces.

Crops to plant:

Blackberries, currant bushes, garlic, gooseberries, raspberries, and strawberries.

Harvest now:

Apples, aubergines, beetroots, Brussels sprouts, calabrese, carrots, celeriac, celery, chillies, courgettes, cucumbers, Florence fennel, French and runner beans, Jerusalem artichokes, kale, kohl rabi, leeks, lettuces, maincrop potatoes, onions and shallots, pears, peas, peppers, plums, pumpkins, radishes, raspberries, spinach, squashes, strawberries, summer cabbages and cauliflowers, swedes, sweetcorn, Swiss chard, tomatoes, and turnips.

Attractive seedheads

Many plants, such as *Phlomis tuberosa* (*right*) and grasses (*see p.224–225*), have attractive seedheads. You can leave these uncut in the garden for winter where they will add structure. Or, you can cut and dry some for an indoor winter display.

Clearing fallen leaves not only keeps the garden tidy but also prevents them from smothering lawns and other plants. Use fallen leaves to make leaf mould, an excellent soil improver, by keeping them in plastic bags for a year to slowly rot down.

Plants growing in containers can be damaged by cold, wet compost that is poorly drained. Raising pots off the ground using "pot feet" (*shown right*), which are available from garden centres, ensure containers drain more freely. They also keep pots raised above any puddles that may form around their bases.

New deciduous hedges, such as beech and hawthorn, can be planted cheaply using bare-root plants between now and late winter. Dig a planting trench, removing any weeds, and improve the soil by adding garden compost. Space the plants 30–60cm (1–2ft) apart and water them in well.

Vegetable crops grown under cover, such as tomatoes, aubergines, peppers, cucumbers, and chillies that have finished cropping can now be removed and the spent plants composted. Green tomatoes can be ripened by placing them in a bag with a banana – the banana releases a vapour that causes nearby fruits to mature. Peppers and chillies won't ripen any further but can be eaten green; immature aubergines and cucumbers are best composted.

Creating habitat areas in the garden is an effective way to attract beneficial wildlife, such as birds, frogs, and hedgehogs, at this time of year. Try to leave some areas untended – a log pile, an area of longer grass, leaves under hedges, an untidy area behind the compost heap – as habitats and shelter for wildlife. If having a bonfire, check it for hiding animals before lighting.

Shortening tall stems on climbing roses helps to prevents them and their support being damaged by strong winds between now and winter, when they are pruned (*see p.309*). Cut back only the tall, thin stems produced this summer, plus any weaker growth.

Prepare greenhouses for winter by removing any shading material used in summer and composting any plants you don't intend to keep. To protect against frosts, line the inside with bubble plastic. This can be held in place using drawing pins in wooden greenhouses or special clips for aluminium ones. On sunnier days, open the windows for a few hours to provide ventilation.

Forking the soil between plants will bring pests to the surface, where birds will find them, and will help to loosen and aerate the earth. Remove any large stones and weeds, and mulch around any slightly tender or newly planted shrubs or perennials.

Dig over empty vegetable beds and prepare the soil in time for spring before it becomes too wet or frozen. Dig over the area to a fork's depth and incorporate plenty of well-rotted garden compost or farmyard manure. Remove any weeds and level the soil surface afterwards.

Large tender plants that can't be brought under cover, such as bananas, ginger lilies, and tree ferns need protection from frost when left outside over winter. Wrap them completely using garden fleece, hessian, or straw, held in place by garden twine or chicken wire. Check after periods of bad weather to ensure the protection is still in place and re-secure it if necessary.

Repotting container-grown trees, shrubs, and fruit bushes

1 If a tree or shrub has grown too large for its pot and is looking poorly, it's time to repot it. Water the plant well to loosen the soil, and ease it from the pot. You may find it easier to lay the pot on its side.

Moving tender plants under cover is the safest way to protect them from frost. A frost-free greenhouse or conservatory would be ideal, but as most plants are dormant at this time, they can also be kept in sheds and garages.

Removing the yellowing leaves from Brussels sprout stems helps to prevent disease. Now is also the time to support these top-heavy plants by inserting canes or by mounding soil at the base of their stems, known as "earthing up".

Covering bare soil with black plastic is a useful way to keep it workable for spring. Any bare soil can be covered, which prevents it becoming too wet, and also controls weeds. Make sure the plastic is securely weighed down.

3 Remove any dead roots – look for any that are dry, crumbly, or show signs of mould. Also check for soil borne pests, such as vine weevil grubs.

4 Replant into a larger pot with good drainage. Add soil-based compost in the base and stand the rootball on top. Fill around it with more compost so that the plant is at its original depth and 5cm (2in) below the rim. Water it thoroughly.

2 Using your hands, carefully remove some of the outermost soil from the rootball to expose the roots. Take care not to disturb the main part of the rootball.

Late autumn

As the days continue to shorten and temperatures fall, make the most of the time you can spend outside in the garden. The soil will stay warm for several weeks to come, making this a good time to choose new plants, and to plan and make changes to your planting schemes.

Essential jobs:

* Plant tulip bulbs (*see p.271*)
* Plant new bare-root ornamental and fruiting trees and shrubs (*see p.272*).
* Protect fruit trees from pests using grease bands (*see p.272*).
* Lift and divide overgrown aquatic plants (*see p.273*).
* Provide support for taller winter crops, such as Brussels sprouts and kale (*see p.273*).
* Prune fruit trees to remove cankerous growths (*see p.273*).
* Clean and put up bird nesting boxes (*see p.273*).
* Protect terracotta pots from frost damage using bubble insulation.
* Drain small decorative water features until spring.

Last chance to:

* Plant spring-flowered bulbs, such as daffodils (*see p.260*), and winter bedding plants (*see p.263*).
* Insulate greenhouses with bubble plastic (*see p.267*).
* Move smaller tender plants undercover before the hard frosts.

Continue to:

* Clear fallen leaves and make leafmould (*see p.266*).
* Plant new deciduous hedges, such as beech (*see p.266*).
* Dig and weed beds as they become empty (*see p.268*).
* Mulch slightly tender plants outside to protect against frost.
* Compost all plant debris.

Crops to sow:

Under cover: Broad beans

Crops to plant:

Apples, blackberries, blueberries, cherries, currants, figs, garlic, gooseberries, pears, plums, raspberries, and rhubarb.

Harvest now:

Apples, Brussels sprouts, carrots, celeriac, celery, Jerusalem artichokes, kale, kohl rabi, leeks, maincrop potatoes, parsnips, radishes, spinach, summer cabbages, swedes, Swiss chard, and turnips.

Watch out for:

* Grey mould on fruit and vegetables – remove infected growth.

Tulip time

Now is the best time to plant
tulips as the colder soil will mean
that *tulip fire*, which is a disease
fatal to the plants, is less likely to
spread. Plant the bulbs to a depth
of three times their height, spaced
a couple of inches apart. Bulbs in
pots can be planted more closely.

Planting bare-root trees and shrubs

1 Dig a hole that's wide enough for the roots to be spread out, and deep enough so the plant is at its original depth. Add garden compost to the base of the hole and drive in a stake if planting a tree or larger shrub.

2 Place the plant into the hole and spread out its roots. To ensure it's planted at its original depth, lay a spade across the hole and position the plant so the top of the soil mark on the trunk or stem is at soil level. Add or remove soil as required.

3 Make sure the tree or shrub is upright and facing the way you want. Once it is, fill the hole gradually using your hands to work the soil in between the roots to avoid any air pockets. Firm the soil down at regular intervals.

4 Once the hole is filled, firm the soil with your feet. If you have inserted a stake, attach the plant to it using an adjustable tie. Water the plant well and mulch around the base with well-rotted garden compost. Keep the plant well watered.

Securing grease bands around the trunks of fruit trees, including apple, pear, plum, and cherry helps prevent various wingless moths from laying their eggs, which hatch into damaging caterpillars on the tree. Use ready-prepared sticky papers, or apply grease directly to the bark, about 45cm (18in) from the base.

Congested pond plants should be taken from the water and divided every few years to encourage flowering and to control their size. Lift them from the pond and use a knife, spade, or fork to split them into healthy sections before replanting.

Taller-growing winter brassicas, including Brussels sprouts and sprouting broccoli can become top-heavy. Stake them to avoid them being blown over, especially if your vegetable plot is in an exposed area. Mulch with compost and protect from pigeons with netting if you haven't done so already.

Mature apple and pear trees often develop "cankers" – areas of dead, sunken bark – on their branches that result in weaker harvests and dead growth. They are caused by a fungal disease and should be pruned out. Cut the affected growth back to healthy tissue and bin or burn it. Seal the cut area with wound paint, which can be bought at garden centres.

Cleaning and putting up bird nesting boxes

1 If you have an existing bird box, take it down and give it a thorough clean to reduce the risk of pests and diseases that affect bird health. Remove any old nesting materials and scrub the box inside and out with boiling soapy water, then leave it to dry.

2 When positioning new bird boxes on a tree or building, site them 2–4m (6–12ft) from the ground, facing east or north to avoid the effects of full sun and strong winds. Ensure that the entrance to the box clear of anything that would block a bird's flight path.

Winter

Signs of Winter

Most plants are dormant at this time of the year, and the garden can look lifeless – even the leaves of evergreens can curl up in the cold. If you're shivering in winter, console yourself with the fact that hardy plants need this cold period in order to flower and fruit when the warmer weather returns.

Winter solstice

The winter solstice occurs around 21st December, and marks the longest night and shortest day of the year. The Northern Hemisphere is now tilted at its farthest away from the Sun, resulting in less heat and lower light levels. At noon on the winter solstice, the sun is the lowest it will be all year.

Day Length

Around the winter solstice there are less than eight hours of daylight per day, and fewer still the further north you go. The passing of the solstice means that days now start to get longer, although that may not seem to be the case at first. Due to the Earth's elliptical orbit, and because actual noon and that incidated by our clocks differs by a few minutes, sunrise will still appear to be getting later for a few weeks.

Weather

Winters in the UK can be variable, and usually bring unsettled and windy weather, caused by depressions and cold fronts moving across the country from the North Atlantic. Winds are at their coldest and strongest now, and can be damaging, while snow is more likely the farther north and higher you go. However, our winters can also be very mild, with southern areas experiencing only occasional frosts.

Temperature

The average UK winter temperature ranges from 1–7°C (34–44°F) but can fall much lower, especially in northern areas and Scotland; -22°C (-8°F) was recorded in Scotland in 1963. Coastal areas are generally the mildest, benefiting from warmer sea air. The coldest month during winter is typically February, while December has the least sunshine.

Plant science

A long period of dormancy is essential to plants that originate from temperate areas, as they can die when forced to continue growing all year. That means winter truly is a time for plants and gardeners alike to rest.

SEEDS

Annual plants overwinter as dormant seed, and one way in which they survive this period is to produce them in abundance, so that some may endure. Seeds vary greatly from plant to plant, and have different methods of surviving winter. Some have a thick outer layer that protects them from cold, while others are tiny, and fall into cracks in the soil, where they are insulated. A common characteristic is that seeds don't contain water, which means their cells can freeze for long periods without being damaged. A cold spell is essential to many seeds, and these won't start germinating until they have experienced temperatures between 5–10°C (41–50°F) for a length of time – known as "vernalization".

PERENNIALS

Most perennial plants die down completely during autumn, and spend winter as dormant roots that are insulated from the coldest conditions by the surrounding soil. Their roots are further protected by containing sugars and starch, rather than water, so are resistant to cell damage caused by freezing (*see right*). Other perennials that retain visible growth above ground do so as tough, weather-resistant buds or shoots that can tolerate the cold. Instead of low temperatures, perennials are most at risk of soil that is saturated for long periods during winter. Plant roots need to breathe, which waterlogged soil prevents. Roots can effectively drown, for which most perennials have no mechanism to survive.

TREES AND SHRUBS

Plants are damaged by freezing temperatures when the water in their cells freezes and expands, causing the cells to burst. This is why frozen plants turn mushy when thawed. To prevent this happening, plants native to colder climates have evolved mechanisms to prevent their cells freezing or to withstand it happening. In some plants, water is pumped out from the fragile cells, leaving a sugary solution that acts like an anti-freeze that is effective to -40°C (-40°F). Some evergreens, such as rhododendron, also change the shape of their leaves, curling them to reduce their exposure to low temperatures. Most deciduous trees and shrubs protect their vulnerable dormant shoots within thick, weatherproof buds.

Tissues rich in starch but free of water avoid damage caused by freezing.

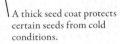

A thick seed coat protects certain seeds from cold conditions.

Sugar- and starch-rich roots resist freezing.

Insulating soil

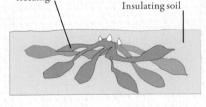

Most perennials are unable to survive in water-saturated soil.

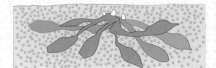

Water leaves the cells in plant tissues and enters the spaces around them.

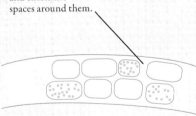

Evergreen leaves can curl inwards and wilt, reducing their exposure to cold conditions.

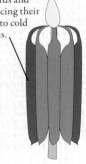

Bedding plants for
Winter colour

Winter bedding plants bring a splash of colour to the garden while other plants are dormant. Plant them in borders and pots in easy view from the house.

1 Polyanthus These primroses flower for several weeks in a wide range of colours if deadheaded.
❀ 10cm (4in) ◣ 10cm (4in)

2 Thyme *Thymus vulgaris* forms a colourful backdrop to flowering plants, especially variegated forms.
❀ 15cm (6in) ◣ 40cm (16in)

3 Silver Dust *Senecio cineraria* is an evergreen perennial that adds colour and texture to displays.
❀ 60cm (2ft) ◣ 60cm (2ft)

4 *Ajuga reptans* An evergreen perennial, use it to provide contrast to flowering bedding.
❀ 1.2m (4ft) ◣ 1.2m (4ft)

5 *Bellis perennis* These double daisies bloom in shades of pink, red, and white from late winter.
❀ 15cm (6in) ◣ 15cm (6in)

6 Winter heathers *Erica carnea* flowers from winter to mid-spring in shades of pink or white. Some forms have golden foliage.
❀ 15cm (6in) ◣ 45cm (18in)

7 Dwarf hardy cyclamen These flower in a wide range of shades, blooming from autumn to winter in all but the coldest weather.
❀ 20cm (8in) ◣ 15cm (6in)

8 Winter pansies and violas These robust plants flower continually from autumn to spring in many shades. Deadhead regularly.
❀ 10cm (4in) ◣ 10cm (4in)

9 Sage *Salvia officinalis* is an evergreen shrub with green, variegated, or purple foliage.
❀ 80cm (32in) ◣ 1m (39in)

10 Winter berry *Solanum capsicastrum* is grown for its round orange berries. It is best planted in a sheltered container.
❀ 40cm (16in) ◣ 40cm (16in)

Helleborus purpurascens

Hellebores

Also known as Lenten or Christmas roses, hellebores (*Helleborus*) flower from mid-winter onwards, in endless shades of white, green, pink, and mauve, with either plain, speckled, or blushing faces. They thrive in shady spots, where those with evergreen foliage give year-round interest. The flowers are downward-facing and best seen at close range, so remove last year's foliage to appreciate them better (*see p.306*). After they have flowered, mulch with well-rotted compost or leaf mould. Hellebores can take time to establish and don't like being moved or divided. They will, however, self-seed readily around the garden, giving you ample free plants.

AT A GLANCE
- ❧ **Plant type** Hardy perennial
- ⚘ **Height** 30–60cm (1–2ft)
- ◖ **Spread** 30–45cm (12–18in)
- ☼ **Aspect** Full or partial shade
- ◉ **Soil type** Fertile and moist

Which to choose

The first hellebores to flower during winter are the Christmas roses, which include *H. purpurascens* (*left*), with its beautiful green and purple flushed flowers.

Christmas roses also include *H. niger*, which produces large white flowers in early winter. These are often flushed with pink or green, and sit above glossy evergreen foliage.

Lenten rose, *H. orientalis*, bears pink-flushed, white blooms from mid-winter. Its many hybrids, *H. x hybridus* (*above*), offer a huge range of shades and variations.

Trees and shrubs for
Winter stems

After shedding their leaves in autumn, many deciduous trees and shrubs reveal colourful and textural stems and branches. Decorative bark can be slow to develop but brightly coloured stems can be easily encouraged by pruning them hard in early spring (*see p.81*).

1 ***Acer griseum*** The paperbark maple tree has attractive coppery bark that peels naturally.
↕ 10m (30ft) ◣ 10m (30ft)

2 ***Cornus sanguinea*** Deciduous common dogwood, such as 'Midwinter Fire' (*see left*) has bright orange or red winter stems.
↕ 3m (10ft) ◣ 3m (10ft)

3 ***Salix alba*** **var.** ***vitellina*** **'Britzensis'** The coral bark willow is a deciduous shrub. When young its stems are red and yellow.
↕ 1.8m (6ft) ◣ 1.5m (5ft)

4 ***Rubus thibetanus*** This clump-forming shrub has chalky white, prickly stems. Good for borders.
↕ 2.5m (8ft) ◣ 2.5m (8ft)

5 ***Corylus avellana*** **'Contorta'** The twisted stems of corkscrew hazel are best appreciated in winter, and are ideal for floral arrangements.
↕ 3m (10ft) ◣ 3m (10ft)

6 ***Cornus alba*** Red-barked dogwood is a deciduous shrub, grown for its vividly coloured stems. There are many varieties to grow.
↕ 3m (10ft) ◣ 3m (10ft)

7 ***Betula utilis*** **var.** ***jacquemontii*** The brilliant white bark of the Himalayan birch tree makes a bold feature in winter, especially when the trees are planted in a group.
↕ 18m (60ft) ◣ 10m (30ft)

8 ***Cornus sericea*** This deciduous dogwood is grown for its stems, which can be dark red or bright lime green, such as 'Flaviramea' (*left*).
↕ 2m (6ft) ◣ 4m (12ft)

9 ***Prunus serrula*** The shiny chestnut-coloured bark of this deciduous tree peels away as it ages, making an attractive winter feature.
↕ 10m (30ft) ◣ 10m (30ft)

Ilex aquifolium 'Bacciflava'

Hollies

The traditional image of holly may be of spiky evergreen leaves and bright red winter berries, but in reality the plant itself is far more varied. Depending on variety, many have brightly variegated foliage; some are viciously spiky, while others are smooth-leaved; and some develop bright yellow berries rather than red. Holly, or *Ilex*, plants are male or female, and only pollinated female plants produce berries. If berries are a must, plant a male and a female holly, or choose a self-fertile variety, such as *Ilex aquifolium* 'J.C. van Tol'. Holly needs little care once established – clipping female plants to shape will result in fewer berries, however.

AT A GLANCE
- ❧ **Plant type** Hardy evergreen shrub
- ♠ **Height** 3–20m (10–70ft)
- 🌢 **Spread** 4–8m (12–25ft)
- ☀ **Aspect** Full sun
- ◉ **Soil type** Moist but well drained

Which to choose

The common holly, *I. aquifolium*, is grown for
its classic red berries, but for something different,
try 'Bacciflava' (*left*), with its vivid yellow fruit.

With variegated spiky leaves, *I. aquifolium*
'Handsworth New Silver' (*above*) is an
attractive female variety. It has red berries.

Smooth-leaved hollies, such as the variegated
I. x *altaclerensis* 'Lawsoniana' (*above*), are ideal
for areas near paths or where children play.

Winter cabbages

Crinkly or smooth-leaved, this leafy crop is a winter treat, especially after frost has sweetened its flavour. It needs space, 50cm (20in) between plants, and is slow-growing, so is best reserved for larger plots. Sow seed under cover in spring or directly outside in summer, keep plants well watered, and feed with high-nitrogen fertilizer in late summer. Harvest the heads once they reach a usable size by cutting through the stem at soil level.

Growing advice

Spring cabbage are sown in summer and are grown in the same way as winter types. Planted 30cm (12in) apart, they are more suitable for smaller plots. Harvest the heads once they reach a usable size.

Cabbage 'Savoy'

AT A GLANCE
- ☙ **Plant type** Hardy annual
- ☀ **Aspect** Partial shade
- ◉ **Soil type** Fertile and moist
- ⌄ **Sow seed** Late spring – early summer
- ◎ **Harvest** Winter – mid-spring

Evergreen shrubs for
Winter interest

Evergreen shrubs provide year-round structure and colour in the garden, and are especially valuable in winter when other plants have died back. Use them as hedging or in mixed borders.

1 **Eleaganus x ebbingei 'Gilt Edge'** Ideal for borders, this shrub has boldly variegated foliage.
🌱 4m (12ft) ◭ 4m (12ft)

2 **Osmanthus heterophyllus 'Aureomarginatus'** Known as false holly due to its foliage, it has fragrant white flowers in autumn.
🌱 2.5m (8ft) ◭ 3m (10ft)

3 **Fatsia japonica** This exotic-looking plant produces large heads of white flowers in autumn.
🌱 4m (12ft) ◭ 4m (12ft)

4 **Phormium cookianum** The slender leaves of these plants come in a wide range of colours.
🌱 2m (6ft) ◭ 3m (10ft)

5 **Aucuba japonica** Female plants of spotted laurel bear red berries in autumn if pollinated by a male. 3m (10ft) ◭ 3m (10ft)

6 **Hebe 'Red Edge'** The red-edged leaves of this compact plant are attractive in winter.
🌱 45cm (18in) ◭ 60cm (24in)

7 **Mahonia japonica** This spiky shrub comes into its own in winter, when its striking foliage is complemented by yellow flowers.
🌱 2m (6ft) ◭ 3m (10ft)

8 **Leucothoe fontanesiana 'Rainbow'** This colourful shrub has an attractive arching habit, and bears white flowers during spring.
🌱 1.5m (5ft) ◭ 2m (6ft)

9 **Euonymus fortunei 'Emerald 'n' Gold'** This low-maintenance shrub is ideal for ground cover.
🌱 60cm (2ft) ◭ 90cm (3ft)

10 **Picea pungens** A dense conifer with blue needles, it looks especially good when planted alongside winter heathers.
🌱 15m (50ft) ◭ 5m (15ft)

Hamamelis mollis

Witch hazels

With their distinctive yellow, orange, or red flowers, borne on bare stems, and heady, spicy scent, witch hazels (*Hamamelis*) are a winter treat. Many also develop colourful autumn foliage, giving a second season of interest. They have a broad, spreading habit, so are best in larger gardens, and will grow in partial shade, but flower more freely in full sun. Dig in organic matter when planting, and mulch in early spring to conserve moisture. Established shrubs need little care but new plants should be initially protected from frost using fleece.

AT A GLANCE
- ❧ **Plant type** Hardy shrub
- ⚘ **Height** 4–5m (12–15ft)
- ◺ **Spread** 2.5–5m (8–15ft)
- ☀ **Aspect** Full sun or partial shade
- ◉ **Soil type** Neutral to acid, moist but free draining

Which to choose

All witch hazels have scented flowers, but those of *H. mollis*
(*see left*) are especially fragrant and fill the air with a peppery
sweet aroma. Other species are equally worth choosing, however.

H. x *intermedia* flowers from early to mid-winter, and is
often the first witch hazel to bloom. There are many varieties
to consider, including copper-flowered 'Jelena' (*above*).

H. *japonica* (*above*) flowers from mid- to late winter, and is
the latest-blooming witch hazel. It is less widely available than
many other choices but has beautiful pale yellow flowers.

Make: A raised bed

Raised beds are ideal for growing vegetables and can be built to suit your needs. Their soil warms quickly in spring, giving your crops a useful head start. Raised beds are ideal if you have limited space.

YOU WILL NEED
* **Materials:**
Pressure-treated timber planks
Treated wooden stakes
Soil and garden compost
* **Tools:**
Cordless screwdriver
Lump hammer
Spade or shovel

2 Place the frame in position and hammer wooden stakes into the soil, one at each corner. Do not fix the frame to the stakes yet, as it needs to be removed so the soil around it can be levelled.

1 Decide what size bed you want and cut four planks to length to form the sides. Using a drill and screws, join the four sides to make a box, then temporarily nail offcuts of timber across the corners to hold the bed frame square.

3 Remove the bed frame and even out the soil where it will sit to create a level base. Shovel any removed soil into the centre of the bed. Add further soil and compost to start creating the bed.

4 Put the frame back in place, saw off the stakes, and screw the frame to them. Add further planks on top of the frame, until the desired bed height is met, screwing them to the corner stakes.

5 To support larger beds, drive stakes in along the sides and cut the tops off at the right height. Fill the bed with soil that has been improved with compost, rake the surface, then water it.

Galanthus elwesii

Snowdrops

These are among the first plants to flower in
the New Year, and brave the coldest weather
to bear their dainty, white blooms. Botanically
known as *Galanthus*, these small bulbs are best
planted in groups for maximum impact, and
will naturalize under deciduous trees and
shrubs, and in grass. Snowdrops are often sold
"in the green" – in leaf after flowering – and
should be planted in late winter (*see p.306*).
Bare bulbs are available in autumn, but can
dry out, so are best bought early while fresh.

Which to choose

Most snowdrops, like *G. elwesii* (*see right*) and our native *G. nivalis* have
single white flowers with green markings, although there are alternatives.

Although there are various double-flowered varieties, such as
G. nivalis f. *pleniflorus* 'Flore Pleno' , 'Lady Elphinstone' (*above*)
has unusual yellow-green centres, making it a choice snowdrop.

AT A GLANCE
- ❧ **Plant type** Hardy bulb
- ❀ **Height** 10–22cm (4–9in)
- 🌢 **Spread** 5–10cm (2–4in)
- ☀ **Aspect** Partial shade
- ◉ **Soil type** Rich, well drained, and moist.

Sprouting broccoli 'Rudolph'

Sprouting broccoli

Also known as purple sprouting, this crop is grown for its tender flower shoots, which appear over a long period in winter and spring. It is a large, slow-growing, but productive plant and can be grown in smaller plots. Seed is sown under cover in spring or directly outside in early summer. Space the plants 60cm (24in) apart, keep them well watered, and support them individually with canes. The flower shoots should be harvested daily in winter and spring, which encourages more to grow.

Growing advice

Sprouting broccoli is harvested by cutting the shoots along with about 10cm (4in) of stem. The tender young leaves can also be picked.

AT A GLANCE
- ❧ **Plant type** Hardy annual
- ☀ **Aspect** Full sun or dappled shade
- ◉ **Soil type** Fertile and moist
- ↓ **Sow seed** Mid-spring – early summer
- ◎ **Harvest** Winter – mid-spring

Jobs to do:
Winter

Around the garden:
- Put out food and water for birds.
- Clear snowfall from paths, plants, and greenhouse and shed roofs.
- Prevent ponds from freezing.

On the veg patch:
- Warm veg patches using cloches.
- Harvest crops as they mature.

In beds and borders:
- Prune roses and other shrubs before spring arrives.
- Check tree ties and plants.
- Plant snowdrops "in the green".

Winter

With plants now dormant, this is a good time to take a look at your garden, to review this year's harvests, and to make plans for the year ahead. In the garden, brush snow from plants and structures to avoid damage, and prevent ponds from freezing over completely.

Essential jobs:

✶ Prune autumn-fruiting raspberries down to soil level.
✶ Prune wisterias by cutting back stems pruned in summer to two buds (see p.197).
✶ Make an air hole in the ice of frozen ponds (see p.304).
✶ Prune established apple and pear trees (see p.305).
✶ Feed the birds (see p.305).
✶ Move established shrubs while dormant (see p.305)
✶ Treat garden timber with wood preservative (see p.306).
✶ Prune deciduous trees and shrubs (see p.306).
✶ Prune flowering shrubs, group 2 and 3 clematis, and climbing roses (see p.309).

Last chance to:

✶ Winter prune gooseberries and fruiting currants (see p.191) and wisteria (see p.197).
✶ Plant bare-root trees, shrubs, and fruit bushes (see p.272).

Continue to:

✶ Support tall brassica crops, such as Brussels sprouts (see p.273).
✶ Put up new bird boxes before spring (see p.273).
✶ Clear snow from the tops of greenhouses and cold frames.
✶ Knock heavy snowfall from shrubs, especially evergreens.
✶ Keep access paths and drives clear of snow and ice.

Watch out for:

✶ Wind and snow damage on trees and shrubs – prune back affected growth.

Crops to sow:

Early winter – under cover:
Broad beans

Late winter – under cover:
Broad beans, Brussels sprouts, celeriac, celery, leeks, peas, and radishes.

Crops to plant:

Apples, blackberries, blueberries, cherries, currants, figs, garlic, gooseberries, pears, plums, raspberries, and rhubarb.

Harvest now:

Early winter:
Brussels sprouts, carrots, celeriac, celery, Jerusalem artichokes, kale, leeks, maincrop potatoes, parsnips, spinach, swedes, Swiss chard, and winter cabbages.

Late winter:
Celeriac, kale, leeks, parsnips, sprouting broccoli, and winter cabbages.

Plan ahead

Now that most leaves have fallen
and perennials have died back,
take time to review your borders.
See where there are gaps, or if
plants are in the wrong place, and
decide what changes you want to
make. Browse through catalogues
and choose new plants and crops
you want to grow.

Winter crops can be harvested as needed, as most stop growing during cold periods and keep well outside. If the weather is especially wet or your soil is heavy, root crops may start to rot, so should be lifted and stored under cover. Brussels sprouts and winter cabbages benefit from cold periods, and tasty sweeter after being frosted.

To prevent ponds from freezing over float a ball on the surface to help maintain an air hole, which is vital to fish and aquatic wildlife. If the water has frozen, melt a hole in the ice by sitting a saucepan filled with boiling water on the surface. Don't crack the ice by hand – the shock waves can harm fish.

Regularly feeding garden birds and providing fresh water helps them survive the winter and attracts them to your garden. To feed and attract a wide variety, put out a varied diet of large and small seeds and nuts, as well as fat balls. Hygiene is essential to prevent bird diseases. Discard uneaten food, and clean your bird tables and feeders regularly.

Established apple and pear trees

need pruning every winter. First remove any crossing, weak, diseased, or damaged growth. Then, thin congested growth from the centre of the tree to give it an open "goblet" shape. Reduce the length of vigorous branches by one third to encourage fruit-bearing spurs to develop at their base. Older fruiting spurs should be thinned out if they have become congested.

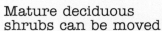

Check tree ties and stakes

on newly planted trees. Replace any ties that are frayed or broken, and make sure that they are not too loose or too tight. Ties that are too tight will damage the trunk. If the stake is loose or broken, hammer it in further or replace it.

Mature deciduous shrubs can be moved

while they are dormant. Dig soil from around the shrub to create as large and intact a rootball as possible. Plant it in its new spot, firm the soil well with your feet, and keep it very well watered.

Cutting back the old leaves from evergreen winter-flowering hellebores (*left*) and epimediums allows the emerging blooms to be more easily seen. Wait until new shoots appear at the base of the plants, then trim all the old leaves and stems to the ground.

Garden furniture can be cleaned while it's not in use. Allow it to dry completely, and if possible, store it under cover. Now plants have died back or become dormant, this is also a good time to treat timber structures in the garden, including fences and benches, with wood preservative. Choose a dry day.

Installing water butts to collect rainwater

saves water, reducing bills, and allows you to store it where you often need it most. When installing a new water butt, raise it off the ground using a stand or some blocks so a watering can be easily placed under the tap.

Time to prune *While they are dormant is a good time to tidy many deciduous trees and shrubs.*

Deciduous trees and shrubs, including Japanese maples (*see pp.242–245*) and flowering dogwoods can be lightly pruned now. Remove any weak, damaged, or crossing branches, and any showing signs of disease. Cut back any excessively long growth produced last year, aiming to give the tree or shrub a balanced shape. Mulch with compost afterwards.

Neaten lawn edges

Now that overhanging plants have died back, it's a good opportunity to reshape your lawn. Use string, spray paint, or a plank of wood to mark the shape, and cut the edges with a spade or half-moon lawn edger. Do this after a spell of dry weather to avoid damaging your lawn.

Heavy snowfall can damage plants, especially evergreen shrubs and conifers, by weighing down their branches, causing them to snap. If snow builds up over several days, gently knock it off your plants using a broom. Snow build-up can also damage greenhouses, sheds, and garden structures, so clear them also.

Deciduous ornamental grasses that have attractive seedheads or develop colourful autumn foliage, such as miscanthus (above), are often left standing over winter for their ornamental effect. As new growth starts to appear from the base of the plants, cut the tired old stems back to ground level.

Planting new snowdrops just after they have flowered, referred to as "in the green", helps them to establish well. They can be bought this way from mail order nurseries.

Cuttings taken last year will have rooted by now, and be ready to pot on. Groups of cuttings grown in a single pot together should be eased out, carefully separated, and potted on individually. Cuttings rooted singly in pots can be simply potted on into pots a few sizes larger.

Covering the bare soil on vegetable patches with sheets of black plastic or cloches helps to warm the soil early. This gives your crops a head start in spring by allowing you to sow seeds sooner, and encourages quicker growth. This is approach especially useful on heavy clay soils, which are slow to dry out and warm up after winter.

Time to prune Many climbers and shrubs can be pruned now to promote flowers and growth.

Climbing roses are pruned to create a framework of main branches, from which flowering shoots grow each year. Remove any old or weak branches from the main framework to the base, plus any weak new growth. Prune last year's new shoots back to healthy outward-facing buds and tie them in to the plant's support using string.

Shrubs that finished flowering in winter, including witch hazel (*Hamamelis*) and wintersweet (*Chimonanthus*) can be pruned now. Simply remove any dead, damaged, weak, or diseased stems, as well as any that cross over or are growing in the wrong direction. Mulch and feed afterwards to encourage growth.

Floribunda, hybrid tea, and shrub roses are pruned by cutting back all of last year's new growth to healthy, outward-facing buds. Thick old stems should be cut to the base, and any weak new growth should be removed. Cut weak shoots back hard; strong ones only lightly. Aim to give the shrubs an open, vase-like shape over all.

Summer-flowering clematis are pruned according to when they flower. Group 2 clematis that flower in early and late summer are cut back to their uppermost pairs of healthy buds, removing all other growth. Group 3 clematis varieties that flower from midsummer are cut back to buds 30cm (12in) above the ground.

Moss, algae, and soil that accumulate in the joints between paving slabs and block pavers can make the surface slippery and unsightly, so are best removed periodically. Small areas can be tackled by hand using a patio weeder (above), or with a special long-handled wire brush, which are available from garden centres. A jet washer is ideal for cleaning larger areas.

Dahlias stored under cover can now be started into growth. First inspect the tubers for signs of decay or damage, and remove the affected areas. Pot the tubers individually into suitably sized containers, using multipurpose compost. Water them in and grow them on under cover, repotting as necessary. They can then be planted out once the risk of frost has passed.

Planting summer-flowering bulbs, such as gladioli and lilies, under cover now is a good way to give them a head start. This encourages an earlier display, and also helps to protect the vulnerable new shoots from pest damage. If the bulbs are to be planted out into beds later in spring, plant them individually into deep containers of multipurpose compost, to a depth of three times their height. Water them in and grow them on under cover until the risk of frost has passed. To plant container displays, choose a large pot with good drainage. Plant the bulbs as described above, but leave them in their container.

Lawn mowers benefit from a thorough cleaning to remove any build-ups of soil and dried grass from around the blades. Check that the blades are sharp and undamaged, and oil the wheels and rollers. If you have a petrol mower, have it serviced before you resume using it.

Winter colour

As the daytime temperatures begin to increase, many bedding plants grow and flower more freely, and benefit from being fed with high potash fertilizer. They will also require more regular deadheading to maintain their display.

Acknowledgments

Picture credits
(Key: l-left; r-right t-top; b-bottom; c-centre)

The publisher would like to thank the following for their kind permission to reproduce their images:
Alamy Images: 46-47 (Yuriy Brykaylo); 50lb (Dave Marsden); 106tr (Dimitri Vervits); 165rb (Valentyn Volkov); 212lt (Eric Tormey)
Peter Anderson: 11lt (RHS Hampton Court Flower Show, designed by Matthew Childs); 245cc (RHS Chelsea Flower Show, designed by Chris Beardshaw); 285cb (RHS Chelsea Flower Show, designed by Prof Nigel Dunnett and The Landscape Agency).
Alan Buckingham: 18, 106tr, 110–111, 111tr, 149rc, 162–163, 187b, 227rt, 227rb, 272-273cb

Lucy Claxton: 164–165, 278, 300–301
Chauney Dunford: 306lt, 310lt, 311
Getty Images: 143lb
International Rose Test Garden, Portland, Oregon: 318–319 (Bruce Forster)
Brian North: 287rt, 243rc
Rough Guides: 204-205 (Tim Draper)
Juliette Wade: 50rt

Dorling Kindersley would like to thank: Mark Winwood and his models for additional photography.

Proofreading: Constance Novis

Indexer: Jane Coulter